AF591487

ARMIES OF THE BEAR

Orders of Battle

Volume I

Soviet Rifle Divisions 1917 - 1957

Part 3: Rifle Divisions 51 to 75

Michael Avanzini & Craig Crofoot

Published by
TIGER LILY PUBLICATIONS LLC

FOR
ORBAT.COM

2005

Editor

Robert Mcarthur
Orbat.com History Books
rmcarthur@cox.net

Useful URLs

www.orbat.com
www.tigerlilypublications.com

Table of Contents

Introduction

This is the first of a series of volumes coving the complete listing of every Division that was in the ground forces of the USSR during its existence. Especially during the "Cold War" era, many Divisions will be identified for the first time and many others will have their designations as identified by Western intelligence corrected.

Using archival material previously unavailable, we are now able to provide a more detailed understanding of the division's lineage, components, activities, and subordination then ever before, including both pre and post World War II data.

1) Formation raised, the Roman numeral next to the division designation indicates the formation number (i.e. Roman numeral "I" indicates 1st formation).
2) The formation, historical summary, and deactivation/disbanding dates.
3) The time period the division was in the Active Army during World War II. For the European Theater of Operation these dates are 22 June 1941 to 11 May 1945, while in the Far Eastern Theater of Operation it is 9 August 1945 to 3 September 1945.
4) The divisional commanders during World War II.
5) The division's honors and awards it received.
6) The division's honorific tile.
7) The division's component units.
8) The Operations that the Division participated in during World War II.
9) The divisions assignment (front, army and corps), on the first of each month, that the Division was active during the Second World War.

Dates are shown in European format of day, month, and year (29.2.42 = 29 February 1942).

The level of detail included makes this book a valuable reference volume for anyone involved in the research of the Red Army and the Eastern Front, from historian to the serious war gamer.

Michael Avanzini Craig Crofoot

About the Authors

Michael Avanzini is a senior designer in environmental engineering in Long Island, New York. In his spare time he is a researcher and scenario designer for HPS Simulations, a computer war game publisher, and a part time musician. He lives in Commack, New York with his wife and two children.

Craig R. Crofoot is a test technician with the Rayovac Corporation in Madison, Wisconsin. In his spare time, Craig is not only collecting any Soviet-era order of battle, but also other countries as well. He also enjoys other subjects, such as science-fiction and Tom Clancy books.

51st Rifle Division (I)

1st Formation

The Division was formed in July 1919 by order of the commander of forces, of the 3rd Army, which at that time was on the Eastern Front. It was formed from elements of the Special Northern Detachment, the Special Brigade and the Vyza'ma Fortress Brigade. It fought during the Russian Civil War from the Urals to the Lake Baikal area, and then was transferred west to the Crimea. After the war, it was assigned to garrison duty in Odessa as part of the Ukrainian Military District. On the 15th anniversary of its assault on Perekop, it was awarded the Order of Lenin. When the Odessa Military District was formed in October 1939, it was transferred to it. In the beginning of 1940, it was transferred north to the Northwestern Front and took part in the Finnish war, after which it returned to Odessa in April 1940. In June 1940, it took part in the invasion of Bessarabia. On 22 June 1941, the Division was in the 9th Separate Army in the Odessa Military District. It fell back through the Ukraine all the way to Rostov. In January 1942, the Division was moved north to the left flank of Southern Front and played a small part in the Barvenkovo-Lozovaia Operation near Izyum. In May 1942, during the Battle of Khar'kov, it was crushed by the German counterattack (Friderikus) and retreated back to the northern Caucasus area where it disbanded in August, although it was not officially disbanded until 28 November 1942.

Active Dates for the Great Patriotic War

22 June 1941 – 28 November 1942

Division Commanders

21.1.1940 -- 22.10.1941	Brigade Commander Petr Gavrilovich Tsirul'nikov (promoted to General-Major on 5.6.1940)
26.10.1941 – 7.5.1942	General-Major[1] Fedor Grigor'evich Filippov
27.5.1942 – 29.6.1942	Lieutenant Colonel Bimbulat Kavdievich Aliev
30.6.1942 – 16.8.1942	Colonel Petr Vasil'evich Vozovik

Honors and Awards

---

[1] Of Technical Forces.

1.11.1920	Awarded the Honorific designation "Perekop"
14.9.1921	Awarded the Honorific designation "in the name of the Moscow City Council"
22.9.1921	Awarded the Order of the Red Banner of Labor
1935	Awarded the Order of Lenin

Division Honorific Title

51st Perekop Red Banner Order of Lenin Rifle Division in the name of the Moscow City Council

Divisional Units

23rd Rifle Regiment (I) (formally 151st Rifle Regiment)
287th Rifle Regiment (I) (formally 152nd Rifle Regiment)
348th Rifle Regiment (I) (formally 153rd Rifle Regiment)
263rd Rifle Regiment (from 12.7.1941) (from the 25th Rifle Division)
218th Artillery Regiment (Formally 51st Artillery Regiment) (until 25.1.1942)
300th Artillery Regiment (from 25.1.1942)
225th Howitzer Artillery Regiment (until.11.1942)
277th Separate Antitank Artillery Battalion
231st Antiaircraft Artillery Battery (formally 165th Antiaircraft Artillery Battalion)
774th Mortar Battalion
30th Reconnaissance Battalion
44th Sapper Battalion
50th Separate Signals Battalion
115th Medical Battalion
60th Separate Chemical Defense Company
57th Auto-Transport Company
60th Field Bakery (formally 65th Field Bakery)
159th Field Postal Station (formally 1495th Field Postal Station)
346th Field Cash Office of the State Bank

Operations

Moldavian Army Group Defensive Operation	1.7.1941 - 26.7.1941
Kiev Strategic Defensive Operation	
Tiraspol'-Melitopol' Army Group Defensive Operation	27.7.1941 - 28.9.1941
Donbass-Rostov Strategic Defensive Operation	
Donbass Army Group Defensive Operation	29.9.1941 - 4.11.1941
Rostov Strategic Offensive Operation	
Bol'shekrepinsk Army Group Offensive Operation	17.11.1941 - 27.11.1941
Rostov Army Group Offensive Operation	27.11.1941 - 2.12.1941
Barvenkovo-Lozovaia Army Group Offensive Operation	18.1.1942 - 31.1.1942
The Battle of Khar'kov	12.5.1942 - 29.5.1942
Voronezh-Voroshilovgrad Strategic Defensive Operation	
Valuiki-Rossosh Army Group Defensive Operation	28.6.1941 - 24.7.1942

Assignments during the Great Patriotic War

Date	Front	Army	Corps
22 June 1941	-	9th Separate Army	14th Rifle Corps
1 July 1941	Southern Front	9th Army	14th Rifle Corps
10 July 1941	Southern Front	Front Reserve	14th Rifle Corps
1 August 1941	Southern Front	9th Army	-
1 September 1941	Southern Front	9th Army	-
1 October 1941	Southern Front	9th Army	-
1 November 1941	Southern Front	Front Reserve	-
1 December 1941	Southern Front	9th Army	-
1942			
1 January 1942	Southern Front	9th Army	-
1 February 1942	Southern Front	9th Army	-
1 March 1942	Southern Front	9th Army	-
1 April 1942	Southern Front	9th Army	-
1 May 1942	Southern Front	9th Army	-
1 June 1942	Southern Front	9th Army	-
1 July 1942	Southwestern Front	9th Army	-
1 August 1942	North Caucasian Front	9th Army	-

51st Rifle Division (II)

2nd Formation

The Division was formed on 15 April 1943 from the 15th Rifle Brigade in the Moscow Military District and assigned to the 3rd Reserve Army. It spent three months training while in reserve and then, in July 1943, was sent to 21st Army in Western Front. The Division participated in the Smolensk Operation advancing toward Orsha. After a short rest back in the Reserves, it was transferred first to 2nd Baltic Front in October, and then to 1st Baltic Front in November. With the 1st Baltic Front, the Division was assign to 4th Shock Army and in June 1944 it participated in the Byelorussian Strategic Offensive Operation, winning its honorific designation "Vitebsk" for helping in its liberation. For its actions during the offensive it also won the Order of the Red Banner. During September 1944, the Division took part in the offensive operations in the Baltic, advancing into Latvia and Lithuania and helping in the capture of Shyaulyai. For these actions, the Division was rewarded with the Order of Suvorov II Class. In December 1944, it was transferred to 49th Army in the 2nd Byelorussian Front and participated in the East Prussian Operation. It was transferred to the 3rd Byelorussian Front in February and remained fighting in East Prussia until the end of the war. After the war, the Division was transferred to the East-Siberian Military District and assigned to the 124th Rifle Corps by November 1945. There is no information on the Division after this point, so it is highly probable that the Division was disbanded early in 1946.

Active Dates for the Great Patriotic War

12 July 1943 - 23 July 1943
1 August 1943 - 25 September 1943
14 October 1943 - 9 May 1945

Division Commanders

15.4.1943 - 23.7.1943	Colonel Petr Sergeyevich TELKOV
24.7.1943 - 9.5.1945	Colonel Aleksey Yakovlevich KHVOSTOV

Honors and Awards

10.6.1944	Awarded the Honorific designation "Vitebsk"
23.7.1944	Awarded the Order of the Red Banner
22.10.1944	Awarded the Order of Suvorov II Class

Division Honorific Title

51st Vitebsk Red Banner Order of Suvorov Rifle Division

Divisional Units

23rd Rifle Regiment (II)
287th Rifle Regiment (II)
348th Rifle Regiment (II)
300th Artillery Regiment (awarded the Order of the Red Banner)
91st Separate Antitank Artillery Battalion
30th Reconnaissance Company
44th Sapper Battalion
207th Separate Signals Battalion (formally 653rd Sep. Signals Company)
115th Medical Battalion
60th Separate Chemical Defense Company
125th Auto-Transport Company
309th Field Bakery
84th Veterinary Field Hospital
1628th Field Postal Station
34th Field Cash Office of the State Bank (formally 1657th Field Cash Office)

Operations

Operation	Dates
Smolensk Strategic Offensive Operation	
Spas-Demensk Army Group Offensive Operation	7.8.1943 – 20.8.1943
Yelnia-Dorogobuzh Army Group Offensive Operation	28.8.1943 – 6.9.1943
Smolensk-Roslavl' Army Group Offensive Operation	15.9.1943 – 2.10.1943
Byelorussian Strategic Offensive Operation	
Gorodok Army Group Offensive Operation	13.12.1943 -31.12.1943
Byelorussian Strategic Offensive Operation	
Vitebsk-Orsha Army Group Offensive Operation	23.6.1944 – 28.6.1944
Baltic Strategic Offensive Operation	
Riga Army Group Offensive Operation	14.9.1944 – 24.10.1944
Memel Army Group Offensive Operation	27.9.1944 – 24.11.1944
East Prussian Strategic Offensive Operation	
Mlawo-Elbing Army Group Offensive Operation	14.1.1945 – 26.1.1945

Assignments during the Great Patriotic War

Date	Front	Army	Corps
1 May 1943	STAVKA Reserves	3rd Reserve Army	-
1 June 1943	STAVKA Reserves	3rd Reserve Army	-
1 July 1943	STAVKA Reserves	3rd Reserve Army	-

Date	Front	Army	Corps
1 August 1943	Western Front	21st Army	61st Rifle Corps
1 September 1943	Western Front	21st Army	61st Rifle Corps
1 October 1943	STAVKA Reserves	-	-
1 November 1943	2nd Baltic Front	22nd Army	-
1 December 1943	1st Baltic Front	4th Shock Army	-
1944			
1 January 1944	1st Baltic Front	4th Shock Army	22nd Guards Rifle Corps
1 February 1944	1st Baltic Front	4th Shock Army	22nd Guards Rifle Corps
1 March 1944	1st Baltic Front	4th Shock Army	91st Rifle Corps
1 April 1944	1st Baltic Front	4th Shock Army	-
1 May 1944	1st Baltic Front	4th Shock Army	83rd Rifle Corps
1 June 1944	1st Baltic Front	4th Shock Army	83rd Rifle Corps
1 July 1944	1st Baltic Front	Front Reserves	22nd Guards Rifle Corps
1 August 1944	1st Baltic Front	Front Reserves	22nd Guards Rifle Corps
1 September 1944	1st Baltic Front	4th Shock Army	22nd Guards Rifle Corps
1 October 1944	1st Baltic Front	6th Guards Army	22nd Guards Rifle Corps
1 November 1944	1st Baltic Front	6th Guards Army	22nd Guards Rifle Corps
1 December 1944	1st Baltic Front	Front Reserves	-
1945			
1 January 1945	2nd Byelorussian Front	49th Army	-
1 February 1945	2nd Byelorussian Front	Front Reserves	124th Rifle Corps
1 March 1945	3rd Byelorussian Front	3rd Army	124th Rifle Corps
1 April 1945	3rd Byelorussian Front	Front Reserves	124th Rifle Corps
1 May 1945	3rd Byelorussian Front	50th Army	124th Rifle Corps

52nd Rifle Division (I)

1st Formation

The Division was formed in 1935 in the city of Kalinkovichi (near Mozyr) in the Moscow Military District. Sometime between then and September 1939, it was transferred to the Byelorussian Military District. It took part in the invasion of Poland in September 1939 and the war with Finland in 1939/40. On 22 June 1941, the Division was in the 14th Army in the Northern Front station in the area around Murmansk. It spent the summer defending and counterattacking the German efforts at capturing Murmansk. By the end of September, the Germans failed in there bid to capture the city. For recognition of its actions during the summer and fall of 1941, the Division was awarded "Guards" status on 26 December 1941 and renamed 10th Guards Rifle Division.

Active Dates for the Great Patriotic War

22 June 1941 - 26 December 1941

Division Commanders

29.11.1939 - 27.7.1941	Brigade Commander Nikolai Nikolaevich NIKISHIN
28.7.1941 - 1.10.1941	Colonel Georgii Aleksandrovich VESCHEZERSKII
2.10.1941 - 26.12.1941	Colonel Mikhail Kazimirovich PASHKOVSKII

Honors and Awards

7.4.1940	Awarded the Order of the Red Banner

Division Honorific Title

52nd Rifle Division

Divisional Units

units were awarded their "Guards" designation on 25.2.1942)

	Becomes
58th Rifle Regiment (I) (formally 154th Rifle Regt)	24th Guards Rifle Regiment
112th Rifle Regiment (I)	28th Guards Rifle Regiment

(formally 155th Rifle Regt)	
205th Rifle Regiment (I) (formally 156th Rifle Regt)	35th Guards Rifle Regiment
158th Artillery Regiment (formally 52nd Art Regt)	29th Guards Artillery Regiment
208th Howitzer Artillery Regiment (until the fall 1941, date unknown)	
54th Separate Antitank Artillery Battalion	14th Guards Sep. AT Artillery Bn.
314th Separate Antiaircraft Artillery Battalion	4th Guards Sep. AA Artillery Battery (until 4.6.1943)
62nd Reconnaissance Battalion	13th Guards Reconnaissance Co.
29th Sapper Battalion	Guards Sapper Battalion
7th Separate Signals Battalion	82nd Guards Sep. Signals Bn.
37th Medical Battalion	481st Medical Battalion
61st Auto-Transport Battalion	499th Auto-Transport Co
191st Mobile Field Bakery	609th Field Bakery
42nd Veterinary Field Hospital	569th Veterinary Field Hospital
141st Divisional Artillery Workshop Battalion	no change
105th Field Postal Station	no change
201st Field Cash Office of the State Bank	no change

Operations

Artic Karelia Strategic Defensive Operation	
Murmansk-Kandalaksha Army Group Defensive Operation	29.6.1941 – 19.9.1941

Assignments during the Great Patriotic War

Date	Front	Army	Corps
22 June 1941	Northern Front	14th Army	-
1 July 1941	Northern Front	14th Army	-
10 July 1941	Northern Front	14th Army	-
1 August 1941	Northern Front	14th Army	-
1 September 1941	Karelian Front	14th Army	-
1 October 1941	Karelian Front	14th Army	-
1 November 1941	Karelian Front	14th Army	-
1 December 1941	Karelian Front	14th Army	-

52nd Rifle Division (II)

2nd Formation

The Division was formed on 1 March 1942 from cadre of the 5th Sapper Brigade in Kolomna in the Moscow Military District. For more then three months, it spent its time completing its formation and training before being assigned to the 2nd Reserve Army in June. In July, it was sent to 30th Army in Kalinin Front, which in August was transferred to Western Front. In late December 1942, the Division was transferred south to the Southwestern Front were it participated in Operation "Gallop" which was part of the Voronezh-Khar'kov Strategic Offensive Operation. It was overrun and pushed back with the rest of the Soviet forces by von Manstein's "backhand blow". With the lull in the action during the spring of 1943, the Division was now assigned to 57th Army in Southwestern Front. During the late summer, it participated in the Donbass Strategic Offensive Operation, and then after being transferred to Steppe Front, the Lower Dnepr Strategic Offensive Operation. In late September, it was pulled from the front to refit and was assigned for a short while to 69th Army. After refitting, it was sent to the 2nd Ukrainian Front where it was reassigned to 57th Army. In February of 1944, the 57th Army was transferred to 3rd Ukrainian Front and during the spring of 1944, the Division participated in the Dnepr-Carpathian Strategic Offensive Operation, advancing to the Dnestr River near Tiraspol'. In late August, the Soviets launched the Iasi-Kishinev Strategic Offensive Operation which was to knock Romania from the war. The 52nd Rifle Division advanced, with 57th Army, south of Bucharest and then during the Belgrade Strategic Offensive it moved through Bulgaria and into Yugoslavia, helping to capture Belgrade and then advanced into Hungary stopping near Lake Balaton. For its actions during these operations, the Division won its honorific designation and the Order of the Red Banner. After a short, rest the Division was transferred to first 4th Guards Army and then 46th Army and was involved in the battles around Budapest throughout the winter of 1945. During March and April, it participated in the Vienna Offensive Operation, helping in the capture of the city and winning its second honorific designation. Then in late April, after being transferred to 53rd Army it took part in the Prague Strategic Offensive advancing toward Prague and ended the war in Czechoslovakia. After the war in Europe ended, the 53rd Army was sent east to participate in the Manchurian Strategic Offensive Operation. The Division was assigned to 57th Rifle Corps, in 53rd Army, in the Transbaikalian Front and took part in the Khingan-Mukden Army Group Offensive out of Mongolia. After the war, the Division returned to the USSR in October 1945 and remained with the 57th Rifle Corps of the 53rd Army until its disbanding, probably in early 1946.

Active Dates for the Great Patriotic War

20 March 1942 - 26 September 1943
26 October 1943 - 11 May 1945
9 August 1945 - 3 September 1945

Division Commanders

1.3.1942 - 14.4.1942	Lieutenant Colonel Kirill Kochoevich DZHAKHUA
23.4.1942 - 27.8.1942	Colonel Vladimir Semenovich ANDREEV
28.8.1942 - 7.5.1943	Colonel Leonid Ivanovich VAGIN
8.5.1943 - 23.5.1943	Lieutenant Colonel Konstantin Pavlovich KOZACHUK
24.5.1943 - 11.8.1943	Lieutenant Colonel Petr Dmitrievich FADEEV
12.8.1943 - 1.1.1944	Colonel Aleksandr Yakovlevich MAKSIMOV
5.1.1944 - 9.5.1945	Colonel Leonid Mikhailovich MILYAEV (promoted to General-Major on 13.9.1944

Honors and Awards

9.9.1944	Awarded the Honorific designation "Shumlinskaya"
14.11.1944	Awarded the Order of the Red Banner
13.4.1945	Awarded the Honorific designation "Viennese"
26.4.1945	Awarded the Order of Suvorov II class

Division Honorific Title

52nd Shumlinskaya Viennese Red Banner Order of Suvorov Rifle Division

Divisional Units

429th Rifle Regiment
431st Rifle Regiment
439th Rifle Regiment
1028th Artillery Regiment
405th Separate Antitank Artillery Battalion
127th Reconnaissance Company
164th Sapper Battalion
587th Separate Signals Battalion (formally 563rd Sep. Signals Company)
106th Medical Battalion
42nd Separate Chemical Defense Company
527th Auto-Transport Company
371st Field Bakery
842nd Veterinary Field Hospital
1827th Field Postal Station
1150th Field Cash Office of the State Bank

Operations

Rzhev-Sychevka Strategic Offensive Operation	
Sychevka Army Group Offensive Operation	24.11.1942 - 14.12.1943
Voronezh-Khar'kov Strategic Offensive Operation	
Voroshilovgrad Army Group Offensive Operation	29.1.1943 - 18.2.1943
Belgorod-Khark'kov Strategic Offensive Operation	
Belgorod-Khar'kov Army Group Offensive Operation	3.8.1943 - 23.8.1943
Lower Dnepr Strategic Offensive Operation	
Kremenchug Army Group Offensive Operation	26.9.1943 - 10.10.1943
Krivoi Rog Army Group Offensive Operation	10.12.1943 - 19.12.1943
Dnepr-Carpathian Strategic Offensive Operation	
Bereznegovatoye-Snigirevka Army Group Operation	6.3.1944 - 18.3.1944
Odessa Army Group Offensive Operation	26.3.1944 - 14.4.1944
Iasi-Kishinev Strategic Offensive Operation	
Kishinev-Izmail Army Group Offensive Operation	20.8.1944 - 29.8.1944
Belgrade Strategic Offensive Operation	14.9.1944 - 24.11.1944
Budapest Strategic Offensive Operation	
Szekesfehervar-Esztergom Army Group Offensive	20.12.1944 - 13.2.1945
Vienna Strategic Offensive Operation	
D'ersk Army Group Offensive Operation	13.3.1945 - 4.4.1945
Assault on Vienna	4.4.1945 - 13.4.1945
Prague Strategic Offensive Operation	
Jihlavo-Benesov Army Group Offensive Operation	6.5.1945 - 11.5.1945
Manchurian Strategic Offensive Operation	
Khingan-Mukden Army Group Offensive Operation	9.8.1945 - 2.9.1945

Assignments during the Great Patriotic War

Date	Front	Army	Corps
1 March 1942	Moscow Military District	-	-
1 April 1942	Moscow Military District	-	-
1 May 1942	Moscow Military District	-	-
1 June 1942	Moscow Military District	-	-
1 July 1942	STAVKA Reserves	2nd Reserve Army	-
1 August 1942	Kalinin Front	30th Army	-
1 September 1942	Western Front	30th Army	-
1 October 1942	Western Front	30th Army	-
1 November 1942	Western Front	30th Army	-
1 December 1942	Western Front	30th Army	-

Date	Front	Army	Corps
1943			
1 January 1943	Southwestern Front	Front Reserves	-
1 February 1943	Southwestern Front (1)	1st Guards Army	
1 March 1943	Southwestern Front	1st Guards Army	6th Guards Rifle Corps
1 April 1943	Southwestern Front	3rd Tank Army	-
1 May 1943	Southwestern Front	57th Army	-
1 June 1943	Southwestern Front	57th Army	-
1 July 1943	Southwestern Front	57th Army	-
1 August 1943	Southwestern Front	57th Army	68th Rifle Corps
1 September 1943	Steppe Front	57th Army	64th Rifle Corps
1 October 1943	STAVKA Reserves	69th Army	76th Rifle Corps
1 November 1943	2nd Ukrainian Front	Front Reserves	35th Guards Rifle Corps
1 December 1943	2nd Ukrainian Front	57th Army	64th Rifle Corps
1944			
1 January 1944	2nd Ukrainian Front	57th Army	64th Rifle Corps
1 February 1944	2nd Ukrainian Front	57th Army	64th Rifle Corps
1 March 1944	3rd Ukrainian Front	57th Army	64th Rifle Corps
1 April 1944	3rd Ukrainian Front	57th Army	64th Rifle Corps
1 May 1944	3rd Ukrainian Front	57th Army	64th Rifle Corps
1 June 1944	3rd Ukrainian Front	57th Army	64th Rifle Corps
1 July 1944	3rd Ukrainian Front	57th Army	64th Rifle Corps
1 August 1944	3rd Ukrainian Front	57th Army	64th Rifle Corps
1 September 1944	3rd Ukrainian Front	57th Army	64th Rifle Corps
1 October 1944	3rd Ukrainian Front	57th Army	64th Rifle Corps
1 November 1944	3rd Ukrainian Front	57th Army	68th Rifle Corps
1 December 1944	3rd Ukrainian Front	Front Reserves	68th Rifle Corps
1945			
1 January 1945	3rd Ukrainian Front	4th Guards Army	68th Rifle Corps
1 February 1945	3rd Ukrainian Front	46th Army	68th Rifle Corps
1 March 1945	2nd Ukrainian Front	46th Army	68th Rifle Corps
1 April 1945	2nd Ukrainian Front	46th Army	18th Guards Rifle Corps
1 May 1945	2nd Ukrainian Front	53rd Army	18th Guards Rifle Corps
1 June 1945	In transport to Far East	53rd Army	-
1 July 1945	In transport to Far East	53rd Army	-
1 August 1945	Trans-Baikalian Front	53rd Army	57th Rifle Corps

Date	Front	Army	Corps
9 August 1945	Trans-Baikalian Front	53rd Army	57th Rifle Corps
3 September 1945	Trans-Baikalian Front	53rd Army	57th Rifle Corps

(1) Not found in the BSSA but assumed to be with the 1st Guards Army of Southwestern Front.

52nd Rifle Division (III)

3rd Formation

There is new information that the Division was re-formed in 1955, by the renaming of the 347th Rifle Division. It was assigned to the Urals Military District, although at the present which Corps Head-quarters it was assigned to remains unclear. Like all of the Divisions formed in 1955, it did not last long however. The Division, as part of the reorganization of the Soviet Army in 1957, became the 52nd Motorized Rifle Division.

Division Commanders

Unknown

Honors and Awards

Division carried over awards from the 347th Rifle Division
None awarded during 1955-1957

Division Honorific Title

52nd Melitopol Red Banner Order of Suvorov Rifle Division

Divisional Units

Currently unknown, but probably same numbered Regiments as previous Division.

53rd Rifle Division (I)

1st Formation

The Division was formed in 1919 and participated in both the Russian Civil War and the Soviet-Polish war of 1920. It was disbanded in 1920.

Active Dates for the Great Patriotic War

None

Division Commanders

Unknown

Honors and Awards

None

Division Honorific Title

53rd Rifle Division

Divisional Units

Unknown

Assignments during the Great Patriotic War

None

53rd Rifle Division (II)

2nd Formation

The Division was formed in 1931 in Pugachev in the Volga Military District. In August/September of 1939 as part of the partial mobilization conducted by the USSR, it was ordered to form two new Divisions, the 148th and 173rd Rifle Divisions, each based around one of the Divisions Rifle Regiments. What remained formed a new 53rd Rifle Division.

Active Dates for the Great Patriotic War

None

Division Commanders

Unknown

Honors and Awards

8.7.1937	Awarded the Honorific designation "in the name of F. Engels"

Division Honorific Title

53rd Rifle Division in the name of F. Engels

Divisional Units

157th Rifle Regiment
158th Rifle Regiment
159th Rifle Regiment
53rd Artillery Regiment

Assignments during the Great Patriotic War

None

53rd Rifle Division (III)

3rd Formation

The Division was formed in September 1939 from what remained of the original 53rd Rifle Division probably based around the 157th Rifle Regiment. On 22 June 1941 the Division was part of the 21st Army in STAVKA Reserve concentrating in the area of Gomel. By the beginning of July it was transferred to 13th Army and station south of Orsha on the Dnepr River defensive line. The Division was pushed back when Guderian's 2nd Panzergruppe crossed the Dnepr, with part of the Division trapped at Mogilev. While it was devastated during the Battle of Smolensk, portions of the Division escaped to reform under 43rd Army of Reserve Front during September. Having lost the 110th Rifle Regiment, the Division received the 475th Rifle Regiment in its place. It remained with 43rd Army throughout the defense of Moscow, avoiding being caught in the encirclement at Vyaz'ma. It then went on to participate in the counteroffensive during the winter of 1941/42. After spending a mostly quite time for the rest of 1942, in February of 1943, the Division was sent south to the 1st Guards Army of Southwestern Front. In late July 1943, it participated in the Izyum-Barvenkovo Offensive, again taking heavy losses. The Division was sent to STAVKA Reserves to rebuild, and returned in time to participate in the Lower Dnepr Strategic Offensive Operation with Steppe Front (renamed the 2nd Ukrainian Front on 20 October 1943). In early 1944, the Division, now with 7th Guards Army, took part in the Uman-Botosani Army Group Operation pushing the Germans back over the Dnerstr River, winning its honorific designation. Then in August 1944, the Division participated in the Iasi-Kishinev Strategic Offensive Operation, knocking Rumania from the war, and advanced through the Carpathian Mountains into Hungary. For its actions during these operations, the Division was awarded the Order of the Red Banner. The Division next participated in the offensive operations around Budapest through the end of 1944 and into 1945. In late March 1945, it took part in the Vienna Strategic Offensive advancing into Czechoslovakia and finally the Prague Offensive, ending the war in the line of contact with the American 3rd Army. It returned to the USSR in the autumn of 1945 and although remaining with the 75th Rifle Corps, the Corps itself was re-assigned to the 57th Army in the Odessa Military District. When the Army was disbanded in 1947, the Division also suffered the same fate at that time.

Active Dates for the Great Patriotic War

2 July 1941 – 3 February 1943
7 March 1943 – 30 July 1943
7 September 1943 – 11 May 1945

Division Commanders

10.12.1940 – 15.7.1941	Colonel Ivan Yakovlevich BARTENEV
16.7.1941 – 23.9.1941	Colonel Fillipp Petrovich KONOVALOV
24.9.1941 – 2.11.1941	Colonel Nikolai Pavlovich KRASNORETSKII
3.11.1941 – 20.9.1942	Colonel Aleksandr Fedorovich NAUMOV (promoted to General-Major on 21.5.1942)
21.9.1942 – 7.4.1943	Colonel Pavel Yefimovich LAZAREV
9.4.1943 – 24.4.1944	General-Major Andrei Yevtikhievich OVSIENKO
4.5.1944 – 11.5.1945	Colonel David Veniaminovich VASILEVSKII (promoted to General-Major on 20.4.1945)

Honors and Awards

Division carried all awards from the previous 53rd Rifle Division

18.3.1944	Awarded the Honorific designation "Novokrainskaya"
15.9.1944	Awarded the Order of the Red Banner
4.6.1945	Awarded the Order of Suvorov II class

Division Honorific Title

53rd Novokrainskaya Red Banner Order of Suvorov Rifle Division

Divisional Units

12th Rifle Regiment
110th Rifle Regiment (until.9.1941)
223rd Rifle Regiment
475th Rifle Regiment (from.9.1941)
36th Artillery Regiment
64th Howitzer Artillery Regiment (until 5.8.1942)
116th Separate Antitank Artillery Battalion
46th Mortar Battalion (from 24.11.1941 to 24.10.1942)
27th Reconnaissance Company
103rd Sapper Battalion
120th Separate Signals Battalion (formally 565th Sep. Signals Company)
244th Medical Battalion (formally 45th Medical Battalion)
94th Separate Chemical Defense Company
85th Auto-Transport Company
26th Field Bakery (formally 155th Field Bakery)
658th Veterinary Field Hospital (formally 193rd Veterinary Field Hospital)
97th Field Postal Station
212th Field Cash Office of the State Bank

Operations

The Battle of Smolensk

Smolensk Army Group Defensive Operation	10.7.1941 – 10.8.1941
Roslavl'-Novozybkov Army Group Offensive	30.8.1941 – 12.9.1941

Moscow Strategic Defensive Operation	
Vyaz'ma Army Group Defensive Operation	2.10.1941 – 13.10.1941
Mozhaisk-Maloyaroslavets Army Group Defensive	10.10.1941 – 30.10.1942
Naro-Fominsk Army Group Defensive Operation	1.12.1941 – 5.12.1941
Moscow Strategic Offensive Operation	
Naro-Fominsk Army Group Offensive Operation	24.12.1941 – 8.1.1942
Rzhev-Vyaz'ma Strategic Offensive Operation	
Mozhaisk-Vyaz'ma Army Group Offensive	10.1.1942 – 28.2.1942
Donbass Strategic Offensive Operation	
Izyum-Barvenkovo Army Group Offensive Operation	17.7.1943 – 27.7.1943
Lower Dnepr Strategic Offensive Operation	
Kremenchug-Pyatikhatki Army Group Offensive	15.10.1943 – 3.11.1943
Krivoi Rog Army Group Offensive Operation	14.11.1943 – 21.11.1943
Aleksabdriia-Znamenka Army Group Offensive	22.11.1943 – 9.12.1943
Krivoi Rog Army Group Offensive Operation	10.12.1943 – 19.12.1943
Dnepr-Carpathian Strategic Offensive Operation	
Kirovograd Army Group Offensive Operation	5.1.1944 – 16.1.1944
Uman-Botosani Army Group Offensive Operation	5.3.1944 – 17.4.1944
Iasi-Kishinev Strategic Offensive Operation	
Iasi-Focsani Army Group Offensive Operation	20.8.1944 – 29.8.1944
Debrecen Army Group Offensive Operation	6.10.1944 – 28.10.1944
Budapest Strategic Offensive Operation	
Szolnok-Budapest Army Group Offensive Operation	29.10.1944 – 10.12.1944
Esztergom-Komarno Army Group Offensive Operation	20.12.1944 – 13.2.1945
Vienna Strategic Offensive Operation	
Assault on Vienna	4.4.1945 – 13.4.1945

Assignments during the Great Patriotic War

Date	Front	Army	Corps
22 June 1941	STAVKA Reserves	21st Army	63rd Rifle Corps
1 July 1941	STAVKA Reserves	21st Army	63rd Rifle Corps
10 July 1941	Western Front	13th Army	61st Rifle Corps
1 August 1941	Reserve Front	43rd Army	-
1 September 1941	Reserve Front	43rd Army	-
1 October 1941	Reserve Front	43rd Army	-
1 November 1941	Western Front	43rd Army	-
1 December 1941	Western Front	43rd Army	-
1942			
1 January 1942	Western Front	43rd Army	-
1 February 1942	Western Front	43rd Army	-
1 March 1942	Western Front	43rd Army	-
1 April 1942	Western Front	43rd Army	-

Date	Front	Army	Corps
1 May 1942	Western Front	43rd Army	-
1 June 1942	Western Front	43rd Army	-
1 July 1942	Western Front	43rd Army	-
1 August 1942	Western Front	43rd Army	-
1 September 1942	Western Front	33rd Army	-
1 October 1942	Western Front	33rd Army	-
1 November 1942	Western Front	33rd Army	-
1 December 1942	Western Front	33rd Army	-
1943			
1 January 1943	Western Front	33rd Army	-
1 February 1943	Western Front	33rd Army	-
1 March 1943	Southwestern Front	1st Guards Army	-
1 April 1943	Southwestern Front	1st Guards Army	6th Guards Rifle Corps
1 May 1943	Southwestern Front	1st Guards Army	6th Guards Rifle Corps
1 June 1943	Southwestern Front	1st Guards Army	-
1 July 1943	Southwestern Front	1st Guards Army	6th Guards Rifle Corps
1 August 1943	STAVKA Reserves	37th Army	-
1 September 1943	STAVKA Reserves	37th Army	57th Rifle Corps
1 October 1943	Steppe Front	7th Guards Army	25th Guards Rifle Corps
1 November 1943	2nd Ukrainian Front	57th Army	64th Rifle Corps
1 December 1943	2nd Ukrainian Front	57th Army	27th Guards Rifle Corps
1944			
1 January 1944	2nd Ukrainian Front	57th Army	-
1 February 1944	2nd Ukrainian Front	7th Guards Army	25th Guards Rifle Corps
1 March 1944	2nd Ukrainian Front	7th Guards Army	25th Guards Rifle Corps
1 April 1944	2nd Ukrainian Front	7th Guards Army	25th Guards Rifle Corps
1 May 1944	2nd Ukrainian Front	7th Guards Army	25th Guards Rifle Corps
1 June 1944	2nd Ukrainian Front	7th Guards Army	25th Guards Rifle Corps
1 July 1944	2nd Ukrainian Front	7th Guards Army	-
1 August 1944	2nd Ukrainian Front	7th Guards Army	-
1 September 1944	2nd Ukrainian Front	7th Guards Army	25th Guards Rifle Corps

Date	Front	Army	Corps
1 October 1944	2nd Ukrainian Front	7th Guards Army	25th Guards Rifle Corps
1 November 1944	2nd Ukrainian Front	7th Guards Army	25th Guards Rifle Corps
1 December 1944	2nd Ukrainian Front	7th Guards Army	25th Guards Rifle Corps
1945			
1 January 1945	2nd Ukrainian Front	7th Guards Army	25th Guards Rifle Corps
1 February 1945	2nd Ukrainian Front	7th Guards Army	25th Guards Rifle Corps
1 March 1945	2nd Ukrainian Front	7th Guards Army	25th Guards Rifle Corps
1 April 1945	2nd Ukrainian Front	46th Army	18th Guards Rifle Corps
1 May 1945	2nd Ukrainian Front	46th Army	75th Rifle Corps

53rd Rifle Division (IV)

4th Formation

There is new information that the Division was re-formed in 1955, by the renaming of the 338th Rifle Division. It was assigned to the Far East Military District, initially as part of the 39th Army, then later as part of the 5th Army. Like all of the Divisions formed in 1955, it did not last long however. The Division, as part of the reorganization of the Soviet Army in 1957, became the 135th Motorized Rifle Division.

Division Commanders

Unknown

Honors and Awards

Division carried over awards from the 338th Rifle Division
None awarded during 1955-1957

Division Honorific Title

53rd Neman Red Banner Rifle Division

Divisional Units

Currently unknown, but probably same numbered Regiments as previous Division.

54th Rifle Division (I)

1st Formation

The Division was formed in mid-1940 in the Leningrad Military District by the reorganization of the 54th Mountain Rifle Division. On 22 June 1941, the Division was in Karelia with the 7th Army defending the Finnish border near Ukhta with the 337th Rifle Regiment in Reboly as part of the Rebol'skoy Operations Group. After falling back during the initial defensive battles along the border, the Division settled down to defending a quiet sector of the front as part of the Kemskaya Operations Group. In April 1942, the Kemskaya Operations Group was renamed the 26th Army, and the Division remained with the Army until the end of 1944. In September 1944, the Division attacked with the rest of the Karelian Front in an offensive designed to knock Finland from the war. After a short rest and refit in STAVKA Reserves at the end of 1944, the Division was assigned to 31st Army and sent south to the 3rd Byelorussian Front. In January 1945, it participated in the East Prussian Operation winning its honorific designation "Masurian" for its actions. In late April, the Division, along with 31st Army was again sent south to the 1st Ukrainian Front in time to participate in the Prague Offensive. The Division ended the war northeast of Prague and became part of the Central Group of Forces occupying Czechoslovakia. As part of this Group, the Division was ordered to disband in June 1945, by STAVKA Order No. 11096 (CGF), dated 29 May 1945, and was disbanded a short time later since it had disappeared from the Soviet order of battle for November 1945.

Active Dates for the Great Patriotic War

22 June 1941 - 14 November 1944
15 December 1944 - 1 April 1945
21 April 1945 - 11 May 1945

Division Commanders

8.10.1940 - 6.4.1942	General-Major Il'ya Vasil'evich PANIN
7.4.1942 - 29.8.1944	Colonel Stepan Pavlovich PERKOV (promoted to General-Major on 1.9.1943)
30.8.1944 - 9.1.1945	Colonel Nikolai Nikolaevich DEGTYAREV
10.1.1945 - 28.1.1945	Colonel Vasilii Georgievich POLYAKOV
29.1.1945 - 9.5.1945	Colonel Gavriil Alekseevich BULANOV

Honors and Awards

23.7.1940	Awarded the Order of Lenin
19.2.1945	Awarded the Order of the Red Banner
5.4.1945	Awarded the Honorific designation "Masurian"
26.4.1945	Awarded the Order of Kutuzov II class

Division Honorific Title

54th Masurian Red Banner Orders of Lenin and Kutuzov Rifle Division

Divisional Units

81st Rifle Regiment (formally 160th Rifle Regiment)
118th Rifle Regiment (formally 161st Rifle Regiment)
337th Rifle Regiment (I) (formally 162nd Rifle Regiment) (until 28.7.1941)
337th Rifle Regiment (II) (from 19.9.1941)
86th Artillery Regiment (Formally 54th Artillery Regiment)
491st Howitzer Artillery Regiment (until 5.10.1941)
58th Separate Antitank Artillery Battalion (I) (until 9.10.1941)
58th Separate Antitank Artillery Battalion (II) (from 12.12.1942)
388th Antiaircraft Artillery Battery (formally 148th Antiaircraft Artillery Battalion) (until 25.5.1943)
366th Mortar Battalion (from 22.10.1941 to 10.10.1942)
142nd Ski Battalion (from 16.1.1942 to 1.5.1942)
200th Ski Battalion (from 16.1.1942 to 1.5.1942)
34th Reconnaissance Company
16th Sapper Battalion
904th Separate Signals Battalion (formally 49th Sep. Signals Bn. 814th Sep. Signals Co.)
29th Medical Battalion
181st Auto-Transport Battalion (until 9.10.1941)
173rd Auto-Transport Company (formally 181 Auto-Transport Company)
161st Veterinary Field Hospital
95th Field Artillery Repair Workshop
117th Divisional Artillery Workshop Battalion
164th Field Bakery (formally 27th Mobile Field Bakery)
192nd Field Postal Station
190th Field Cash Office of the State Bank

Operations

Artic and Karelia Strategic Defensive Operation	
Defensive Operations near Petrozavodsk	1.7.1941 – 10.10.1941
East Prussian Strategic Offensive Operation	
Insterburg-Königsberg Army Group Offensive Operation	14.1.1945 – 26.1.1945
Braunsburg Army Group Offensive Operation	13.3.1945 - 22.3.1945
Prague Strategic Offensive Operation	
Sudeten Army Group Offensive Operation	6.5.1945 – 11.5.1945

Assignments during the Great Patriotic War

Date	Front	Army	Corps
22 June 1941	Northern Front	7th Army	-
1 July 1941	Northern Front	7th Army	-
10 July 1941	Northern Front	7th Army	-
1 August 1941	Northern Front	7th Army	-
1 September 1941	Karelian Front	7th Army	-
1 October 1941	Karelian Front	Kemskaya Operations Group	-
1 November 1941	Karelian Front	Kemskaya Operations Group	-
1 December 1941	Karelian Front	Kemskaya Operations Group	-
1942			
1 January 1942	Karelian Front	Kemskaya Operations Group	-
1 February 1942	Karelian Front	Kemskaya Operations Group	-
1 March 1942	Karelian Front	Kemskaya Operations Group	-
1 April 1942	Karelian Front	Kemskaya Operations Group (designated 26th Army)	-
1 May 1942	Karelian Front	26th Army	-
1 June 1942	Karelian Front	26th Army	-
1 July 1942	Karelian Front	26th Army	-
1 August 1942	Karelian Front	26th Army	-
1 September 1942	Karelian Front	26th Army	-
1 October 1942	Karelian Front	26th Army	-
1 November 1942	Karelian Front	26th Army	-
1 December 1942	Karelian Front	26th Army	-
1943			
1 January 1943	Karelian Front	26th Army	
1 February 1943	Karelian Front	26th Army	-
1 March 1943	Karelian Front	26th Army	-
1 April 1943	Karelian Front	26th Army	-
1 May 1943	Karelian Front	26th Army	-

Date	Front	Army	Corps
1 June 1943	Karelian Front	26th Army	-
1 July 1943	Karelian Front	26th Army	-
1 August 1943	Karelian Front	26th Army	-
1 September 1943	Karelian Front	26th Army	-
1 October 1943	Karelian Front	26th Army	-
1 November 1943	Karelian Front	26th Army	-
1 December 1943	Karelian Front	26th Army	-
1944			
1 January 1944	Karelian Front	26th Army	-
1 February 1944	Karelian Front	26th Army	-
1 March 1944	Karelian Front	26th Army	-
1 April 1944	Karelian Front	26th Army	-
1 May 1944	Karelian Front	26th Army	-
1 June 1944	Karelian Front	26th Army	-
1 July 1944	Karelian Front	26th Army	-
1 August 1944	Karelian Front	26th Army	-
1 September 1944	Karelian Front	26th Army	132nd Rifle Corps
1 October 1944	Karelian Front	26th Army	132nd Rifle Corps
1 November 1944	Karelian Front	26th Army	132nd Rifle Corps
1 December 1944	STAVKA Reserves	26th Army	-
1945			
1 January 1945	3rd Byelorussian Front	31st Army	-
1 February 1945	3rd Byelorussian Front	31st Army	71st Rifle Corps
1 March 1945	3rd Byelorussian Front	31st Army	71st Rifle Corps
1 April 1945	3rd Byelorussian Front	31st Army	71st Rifle Corps
1 May 1945	1st Ukrainian Front	31st Army	71st Rifle Corps
1 June 1945	Central Group of Forces	31st Army	71st Rifle Corps

54th Rifle Division (II)

2nd Formation

There is new information that the Division was re-formed in 1955, by the renaming of the 341st Rifle Division. It was assigned to the Northern Military District, although at present, which Army or Corps Head-quarters it was assigned to remains unclear. Like all of the Divisions formed in 1955, it did not last long however. The Division, as part of the reorganization of the Soviet Army in 1957, became the 54th Motorized Rifle Division.

Division Commanders

Unknown

Honors and Awards

Division carried over awards from the 341st Rifle Division
None awarded during 1955-1957

Division Honorific Title

54th Rifle Division

Divisional Units

Currently unknown, but probably same numbered Regiments as previous Division.

55th Rifle Division (I)

1st Formation

The Division was formed in 1925 in Kursk in the (at the time) Moscow Military District as a territorial Division. In July 1938, the Kursk region was transferred to the Orel Military District. In August/
September of 1939, as part of the partial mobilization conducted by the USSR, it was ordered to form two new Divisions, first the 185th, and then the 113th Rifle Divisions, each based around one of the Divisions Rifle Regiments. What remained formed a new 55th Rifle Division.

Active Dates for the Great Patriotic War

None

Division Commanders

Unknown

Honors and Awards

12.1.1926	Awarded the Honorific designation "Kursk"
26.7.1926	Awarded the Honorific designation "in the name of K.E. Voroshilov"

Division Honorific Title

55th Kursk Rifle Division in the name of K.E. Voroshilov

Divisional Units

163rd Rifle Regiment
164th Rifle Regiment
165th Rifle Regiment
55th Artillery Regiment

Assignments during the Great Patriotic War

None

55th Rifle Division (II)

2nd Formation

The Division was formed in September 1939 from what remained of the original 55th Rifle Division probably based around the 163rd Rifle Regiment. Even though it was still training as a new Division, it took part in the invasion of Poland in September 1939 as part of the Byelorussian Front, where it remained until June 1940. In June 1940, it took part in the invasion of Lithuania as part of the 24th Rifle Corps, 3rd Army. When it returned to the Western Special Military District in the later half of 1940, it did a tour of duty in the Brest fortress. Afterward, it was assigned to District reserves. On 22 June 1941, the Division was in the 47th Rifle Corps of Western Front Reserves, stationed at Slutsk. It was pushed back across the Dnepr in early July and incorporated into 4th Army's defense along the Sozh River. Transferred to 13th Army and Central Front in late July, the Division fell back toward Kiev when Guderian turned south during August of 1941. In late August, it was transferred to 21st Army in Bryansk Front, but was caught in the German encirclement near Kiev and destroyed. It was officially disbanded on 27 December 1941.

Active Dates for the Great Patriotic War

22 June 1941 - 27 December 1941

Division Commanders

21.2.1940 - 13.7.1941	Colonel Dmitrii Ivanovich IVANYUK
14.7.1941 - 1.10.1941	Colonel Gevork Andreevich TER-GASPARYAN

Honors and Awards

Division carried all awards from the previous 55th Rifle Division

Division Honorific Title

55th Kursk Rifle Division in the name of K.E. Voroshilov

Divisional Units

107th Rifle Regiment (I)
111th Rifle Regiment (I)
228th Rifle Regiment (I)

84th Artillery Regiment
141st Howitzer Artillery Regiment
129th Separate Antitank Artillery Battalion
250th Separate Antiaircraft Artillery Battalion
79th Separate Reconnaissance Battalion
46th Sapper Battalion
21st Separate Signals Battalion
67th Medical Battalion
80th Auto-Transport Battalion
169th Mobile Field Bakery
21st Divisional Artillery Workshop Battalion
117th Field Postal Station
354th Field Cash Office of the State Bank

Operations

The Battle of Smolensk	
Smolensk Army Group Defensive Operation	10.7.1941 - 10.8.1941
Gomel'-Trubchevsk Army Group Defensive Operation	24.7.1941 - 30.8.1941
Kiev Strategic Defensive Operation	
Kiev-Priluki Army Group Defensive Operation	20.8.1941 - 26.9.1941

Assignments during the Great Patriotic War

Date	Front	Army	Corps
22 June 1941	Western Front	Front Reserves	47th Rifle Corps
1 July 1941	Western Front	4th Army	47th Rifle Corps
10 July 1941	Western Front	4th Army	28th Rifle Corps
1 August 1941	Central Front	13th Army	28th Rifle Corps
1 September 1941	Bryansk Front	21st Army	66th Rifle Corps

55th Rifle Division (III)

3rd Formation

The Division was formed on 12 December 1941 at Kuibyshev in the Volga Military District. It spent 3 months forming and training before being assigned to STAVKA Reserves in late March 1942. In April, it was sent north to 11th Army in Northwestern Front and participated in the fighting around the Demyansk pocket until the Germans evacuated the pocket in March 1943. The Division went back into STAVKA Reserves for a short while before being transferred south. It was assigned to Central Front, and during the Battle of Kursk was in the 60th Army defending in the quiet sector directly west of Kursk. The Division was back in STAVKA Reserves during August/September and was again assigned to Central Front in late September with 61st Army. It participated in the Byelorussian Strategic Offensive Operation, pushing the Germans back over the Dnepr River in the area of Kalinkovichi, just south of Gomel. By this time, the Central Front had been renamed the Byelorussian Front. In January 1944, the Division took part in the Kalinkovichi-Mozyr Army Group Operation, helping to liberate Mozyr and winnings its honorific designation. During the Byelorussian Strategic Offensive Operation in late June/July 1944, the Division participated in the later stages of the Operation, pushing the Germans back through Brest and winning the Order of the Red Banner. In late July, the 61st Army with the 55th Rifle Division was sent into STAVKA Reserves to rebuild. In September, the 61st Army was transferred to 3rd Baltic Front and participated in the Baltic Strategic Offensive Operation helping in the capture of Riga. On October 10th, 1944, it was ordered that the 55th Rifle Division be transferred to the Red Banner Baltic Fleet for garrison duties at the new Naval Base in Porkkala, Finland. On 10 December 1944, the Division was renamed the 1st Mozyr'skaya Red Banner Naval Infantry Division, with a tank regiment added to its composition. This Division was disbanded in 1947.

Active Dates for the Great Patriotic War

7 April 1942 – 25 March 1943
10 May 1943 – 30 July 1944
13 September 1944 – 10 October 1944

Division Commanders

12.12.1941 – 10.5.1942	General-Major Ivan Pavlovich SHEVCHUK
11.5.1942 – 21.1.1944	Colonel Nikolai Nikolaevich ZAIYUL'EV
22.1.1944 – 7.10.1944	Colonel Kornei Mikhailovich ANDRUSENKO
8.10.1944 – 10.12.1944	Unknown

Honors and Awards

15.1.1944	Awarded the Honorific designation "Mozyr'skaya"
23.7.1944	Awarded the Order of the Red Banner

Division Honorific Title

55th Mozyr'skaya Red Banner Rifle Division

Divisional Units

107th Rifle Regiment (II)
111th Rifle Regiment (II)
228th Rifle Regiment (II)
84th Artillery Regiment
129th Separate Antitank Artillery Battalion
35th Mortar Battalion (until 9.10.1942)
543rd Reconnaissance Company
46th Sapper Battalion
21st Separate Signals Company (until 28.2.1943)
21st Separate Signals Battalion (from 28.2.1943)
67th Medical Battalion
489th Separate Chemical Defense Company
80th Auto-Transport Company
405th Field Bakery
867th Veterinary Field Hospital
1656th Field Postal Station
1050th Field Cash Office of the State Bank

Operations

Demyansk Army Group Offensive Operation	7.1.1942 - 20.5.1942
Demyansk Army Group Offensive Operation	15.2.1943 - 28.2.1943
Byelorussian Strategic Offensive Operation	
Gomel'sko-Rechitskaia Army Group Offensive Operation	30.9.1943 - 30.10.1943
Gomel'sko-Rechitskaia Army Group Offensive Operation	10.11.1943 - 30.11.1943
Kalinkovichi Army Group Offensive Operation	8.12.1943 - 11.12.1943
Kalinkovichi Army Group Offensive Operation	20.12.1943 - 27.12.1943
Kalinkovichi-Mozyr Army Group Offensive Operation	8.1.1944 - 26.2.1944
Byelorussian Strategic Offensive Operation	
Lublin-Brest Army Group Offensive Operation	18.7.1944 - 2.8.1944
Baltic Strategic Offensive Operation	
Riga Army Group Offensive Operation	14.9.1944 - 24.10.1944

Assignments during the Great Patriotic War

Date	Front	Army	Corps
1 January 1942	Volga Military District	-	-
1 February 1942	Volga Military District	-	-
1 March 1942	Volga Military District	-	-
1 April 1942	STAVKA Reserve	-	-
1 May 1942	Northwestern Front	11th Army	-
1 June 1942	Northwestern Front	11th Army	-
1 July 1942	Northwestern Front	11th Army	-
1 August 1942	Northwestern Front	11th Army	-
1 September 1942	Northwestern Front	11th Army	-
1 October 1942	Northwestern Front	11th Army	-
1 November 1942	Northwestern Front	11th Army	-
1 December 1942	Northwestern Front	27th Army	-
1943			
1 January 1943	Northwestern Front	11th Army	-
1 February 1943	Northwestern Front	11th Army	-
1 March 1943	Northwestern Front	27th Army	-
1 April 1943	STAVKA Reserve	53rd Army	-
1 May 1943	Steppe Military District	53rd Army	-
1 June 1943	Central Front	Front Reserves	-
1 July 1943	Central Front	60th Army	-
1 August 1943	Central Front	70th Army	-
1 September 1943	STAVKA Reserve	61st Army	29th Rifle Corps
1 October 1943	Central Front	61st Army	29th Rifle Corps
1 November 1943	Byelorussian Front	61st Army	29th Rifle Corps
1 December 1943	Byelorussian Front	61st Army	89th Rifle Corps
1944			
1 January 1944	Byelorussian Front	61st Army	89th Rifle Corps
1 February 1944	Byelorussian Front	61st Army	-
1 March 1944	2nd Byelorussian Front	61st Army	-
1 April 1944	2nd Byelorussian Front	61st Army	89th Rifle Corps
1 May 1944	1st Byelorussian Front	61st Army	89th Rifle Corps
1 June 1944	1st Byelorussian Front	61st Army	89th Rifle Corps
1 July 1944	1st Byelorussian Front	61st Army	89th Rifle Corps
1 August 1944	STAVKA Reserve	61st Army	89th Rifle Corps
1 September 1944	STAVKA Reserve	61st Army	89th Rifle Corps
1 October 1944	3rd Baltic Front	61st Army	89th Rifle Corps

55th Rifle Division (IV)

4th Formation

There is new information that the Division was re-formed in 1955, by the renaming of the 343rd Rifle Division. It was assigned to the Kiev Military District, although at present, which Corps or Army Headquarters it was assigned to remains unclear. Like all of the Divisions formed in 1955, it did not last long however. The Division, as part of the reorganization of the Soviet Army in 1957, became the 136th Motorized Rifle Division.

Division Commanders

Unknown

Honors and Awards

Division carried over awards from the 343rd Rifle Division
None awarded during 1955-1957

Division Honorific Title

55th Belostok Red Banner Order of Suvorov Rifle Division

Divisional Units

Currently unknown, but probably same numbered Regiments as previous Division.

56th Rifle Division (I)

1st Formation

The Division was formed on 21 November 1919. It received the honorific "Moscow" on 13 December 1919. It took part in both the Russian Civil War and the Soviet-Polish wars. It was also assigned to put down the Kronstadt mutiny. During the 1920s and 1930s, it was on garrison duty in Pskov, first as a territorial Division, then in 1936 upgraded to a cadre Division. When World War 2 broke out, it was assigned to the Novgorod Army Group (later renamed the 8th Army), but in November 1939, it was transferred north to the Petrozavodsk region and in December 1939 began operations against the Finns. It remained in the region until June 1940 when it took part in the invasion of Estonia. Afterward, it was transferred south to the Western Special Military District. On 22 June 1941, the Division was in the 4th Rifle Corps, 3rd Army in Western Front, stationed in the Grodno region. The 213th Rifle Regiment, which is defending near the town of Sopotskin was quickly overrun by the Germans and destroyed. The rest of the Division was pushed back and eventually trapped in the large encirclement west of Minsk and destroyed by early July. It was officially disbanded on 19 September 1941.

Active Dates for the Great Patriotic War

22 June 1941 - 19 September 1941

Division Commanders

12.6.1941 - 30.6.1941	General-Major Semen Pavlovich SAKHNOV

Honors and Awards

13.12.1919	Awarded the Honorific designation "Moscow"
1928	Awarded the Revolutionary Red Banner

Division Honorific Title

56th Moscow Rifle Division

Divisional Units

37th Rifle Regiment (I) (formally 166th Rifle Regiment)
184th Rifle Regiment (I) (formally 167th Rifle Regiment)

213th Rifle Regiment (I) (formally 168th Rifle Regiment)
113th Artillery Regiment (Formally 56th Artillery Regiment)
247th Howitzer Artillery Regiment
59th Separate Antitank Artillery Battalion
277th Separate Antiaircraft Artillery Battalion
38th Reconnaissance Battalion
79th Sapper Battalion
22nd Separate Signals Battalion
107th Medical Battalion
131st Separate Chemical Defense Company
50th Auto-Transport Battalion
73rd Mobile Field Bakery
188th Field Postal Station
191st Field Cash Office of the State Bank

Operations

Byelorussian Strategic Defense Offensive
Border Defensive Battles 22.6.1941 – 25.6.1941

Assignments during the Great Patriotic War

Date	Front	Army	Corps
22 June 1941	Western Front	3rd Army	4th Rifle Corps
1 July 1941	Western Front	3rd Army	-

56th Rifle Division (II)

2nd Formation

The Division was formed on 26 September 1941 from the 7th Leningrad Rifle Division of the People's Militia in the 42nd Army of Leningrad Front. It was transferred to 55th Army in November 1941 and remained there until March of 1943 when the Division was transferred back to 42nd Army. All this time was spent on the front lines during the siege and the Division saw little action. In January 1944, the Division participated in the Leningrad-Novgorod Strategic Offensive Operation. The Division won its honorific title for the liberation of Pushkin, and ended the offensive with 67th Army near Pskov. During August 1944, with the 1st Shock Army in 3rd Baltic Front, it took part in the Tartu Army Group Offensive advancing into Latvia. In September, back in 67th Army, the Division participated in the Baltic Strategic Offensive Operation, capturing Riga and pushing the Germans back into the Kurland peninsula. The Division spent the rest of the war containing the Germans in Kurland with the 67th and then the 42nd Armies. After the war, it was transferred to the West-Siberian Military District and assigned to the 122nd Rifle Corps. Its fate after this point is unknown at this time, although there is some evidence it remained active until August 1946 when it was reorganized into the 67th Mechanized Division.

Active Dates for the Great Patriotic War

26 September 1941 - 9 May 1945

Division Commanders

22.9.1941 - 8.1.1942	Colonel Iov Sergeevich KUZNETSOV
9.1.1942 - 16.12.1942	Colonel Pavel Karpovich LOSKUTOV
17.12.1942 - 28.7.1944	Colonel Stepan Mikhailovich BUN'KOV (promoted to General-Major on 20.12.1943)
29.7.1944 - 14.10.1944	General-Major Kornei Grigor'evich REBRIKOV
15.10.1944 - 22.2.1945	Colonel Aleksandr Aleksandrovich VOLKOV
25.2.1945 - 9.5.1945	General-Major Ivan Ivanovich USENKO

Honors and Awards

27.1.1944	Awarded the Honorific designation "Puskinskaya"
20.2.1944	Awarded the Order of the Red Banner

Division Honorific Title

56th Puskinskaya Red Banner Rifle Division

Divisional Units

37th Rifle Regiment (II)
184th Rifle Regiment (II)
213th Rifle Regiment (II)
113th Artillery Regiment
59th Separate Antitank Artillery Battalion (from 10.6.1943)
381st Mortar Battalion (until 15.10.1942)
38th Reconnaissance Company
79th Sapper Battalion
22nd Separate Signals Battalion (formally 22nd and 849th Separate Signals Companies)
107th Medical Battalion
131st Separate Chemical Defense Company
114th Auto-Transport Company
341st Field Bakery (formally 73rd Mobile Field Bakery)
189th Veterinary Field Hospital
127th Divisional Artillery Workshop Battalion
494th Field Postal Station
628th Field Cash Office of the State Bank

Operations

Sinyavino Army Group Offensive Operation	19.8.1942 - 10.10.1942
Leningrad-Novgorod Strategic Offensive Operation	
Krasnoye Selo-Ropsha Army Group Offensive Operation	14.1.1944 - 30.1.1944
Kingisepp-Gdov Army Group Offensive Operation	1.2.1944 - 1.3.1944
Tartu Army Group Offensive Operation	10.8.1944 - 6.9.1944
Baltic Strategic Offensive Operation	
Riga Army Group Offensive Operation	14.9.1944 - 24.10.1944

Assignments during the Great Patriotic War

Date	Front	Army	Corps
1 October 1941	Leningrad Front	42nd Army	-
1 November 1941	Leningrad Front	42nd Army	-
1 December 1941	Leningrad Front	55th Army	-
1942			
1 January 1942	Leningrad Front	55th Army	-
1 February 1942	Leningrad Front	55th Army	-
1 March 1942	Leningrad Front	55th Army	-
1 April 1942	Leningrad Front	55th Army	-
1 May 1942	Leningrad Front	55th Army	-

Date	Front	Army	Corps
1 June 1942	Leningrad Front	55th Army	-
1 July 1942	Leningrad Front	55th Army	-
1 August 1942	Leningrad Front	55th Army	-
1 September 1942	Leningrad Front	55th Army	-
1 October 1942	Leningrad Front	Front Reserves	-
1 November 1942	Leningrad Front	55th Army	-
1 December 1942	Leningrad Front	55th Army	-
1943			
1 January 1943	Leningrad Front	55th Army	-
1 February 1943	Leningrad Front	55th Army	-
1 March 1943	Leningrad Front	55th Army	-
1 April 1943	Leningrad Front	42nd Army	-
1 May 1943	Leningrad Front	42nd Army	-
1 June 1943	Leningrad Front	42nd Army	-
1 July 1943	Leningrad Front	42nd Army	-
1 August 1943	Leningrad Front	42nd Army	-
1 September 1943	Leningrad Front	42nd Army	-
1 October 1943	Leningrad Front	42nd Army	-
1 November 1943	Leningrad Front	42nd Army	-
1 December 1943	Leningrad Front	42nd Army	110th Rifle Corps
1944			
1 January 1944	Leningrad Front	42nd Army	110th Rifle Corps
1 February 1944	Leningrad Front	67th Army	110th Rifle Corps
1 March 1944	Leningrad Front	67th Army	110th Rifle Corps
1 April 1944	Leningrad Front	67th Army	110th Rifle Corps
1 May 1944	3rd Baltic Front	67th Army	110th Rifle Corps
1 June 1944	3rd Baltic Front	67th Army	123rd Rifle Corps
1 July 1944	3rd Baltic Front	67th Army	123rd Rifle Corps
1 August 1944	3rd Baltic Front	1st Shock Army	123rd Rifle Corps
1 September 1944	3rd Baltic Front	1st Shock Army	14th Guards Rifle Corps
1 October 1944	3rd Baltic Front	67th Army	122nd Rifle Corps
1 November 1944	Leningrad Front	67th Army	122nd Rifle Corps
1 December 1944	Leningrad Front	67th Army	122nd Rifle Corps
1945			
1 January 1945	Leningrad Front	67th Army	122nd Rifle Corps
1 February 1945	Leningrad Front	67th Army	122nd Rifle Corps
1 March 1945	2nd Baltic Front	Front Reserves	122nd Rifle Corps
1 April 1945	Leningrad Front – Kurland Group of Forces	42nd Army	122nd Rifle Corps

Date	Front	Army	Corps
1 May 1945	Leningrad Front – Kurland Group of Forces	42nd Army	122nd Rifle Corps

56th Rifle Division (III)

3rd Formation

There is new information that the Division was re-formed in 1955, by the renaming of the 342nd Rifle Division. It was assigned to the Far East Military District, although at present, which Army or Corps Head-quarters it was assigned to remains unclear. Like all of the Divisions formed in 1955, it did not last long however. The Division, as part of the reorganization of the Soviet Army in 1957, became the 56th Motorized Rifle Division.

Division Commanders

Unknown

Honors and Awards

Division carried over awards from the 342nd Rifle Division
None awarded during 1955-1957

Division Honorific Title

56th Rifle Division

Divisional Units

Currently unknown, but probably same numbered Regiments as previous Division.

57th Rifle Division (I)

1st Formation

The Division was formed in January 1921 from the 24th "Ekaterinburg" Rifle Division of the Internal Service Forces. In 1924 its honorary designation was changed to Ural and it was made a territorial division in the Volga Military District. In 1931/32 the Division was upgraded to a "cadre" Division and transferred to the Transbaikal Military District. Its rifle regiments were used to form three new rifle divisions, the 65th in Sverdlovsk, 82nd in Perm and the 85th Rifle Division in Chelyabinsk. In August 1939, it was part of the reinforcements used in the battle of Khalkhin-Gol against the Japanese, winning the Order of the Red Banner. In the beginning of 1940, the Division was reorganized as a Motorized Rifle Division.

Active Dates for the Great Patriotic War

None

Division Commanders

Unknown

Honors and Awards

1924	Changed the Honorary designation to "Ural"
1939	Awarded the Order of the Red Banner

Division Honorific Title

57th Urals Red Banner Rifle Division

Divisional Units

80th Rifle Regiment
127th Rifle Regiment
243rd Rifle Regiment
105th Artillery Regiment

Assignments during the Great Patriotic War

None

57th Rifle Division (II)

2nd Formation

There is new information that the Division was re-formed in 1955, by the renaming of the 345th Rifle Division. It was assigned to the Far East Military District, first as part of the 15th Army, then later as part of the 1st Red Banner Army. Like all of the Divisions formed in 1955, it did not last long however. The Division, as part of the reorganization of the Soviet Army in 1957, became the 137th Motorized Rifle Division.

Division Commanders

Unknown

Honors and Awards

Division carried over awards from the 345th Rifle Division
None awarded during 1955-1957

Division Honorific Title

57th Rifle Division

Divisional Units

Currently unknown, but probably same numbered Regiments as previous Division.

58th Rifle Division (I)

1st Formation

The Division was formed in 21 July 1919. After taking part in the Russian Civil War, it was disbanded on 12 May 1921.

Active Dates for the Great Patriotic War

None

Division Commanders

Unknown

Honors and Awards

1919	Awarded the Honorary Revolutionary Red Banner
1920	Awarded the Order of the Red Banner

Division Honorific Title

58th twice Red Banner Rifle Division

Divisional Units

Unknown

Assignments during the Great Patriotic War

None

58th Rifle Division (II)

2nd Formation

The Division was formed in 1932 in the Ukrainian Military District. In May 1935, it was transferred west to the Kiev and Khar'kov Military Districts, with its units split between Cherkassy, Smela and Zolotonosha. In August 1939, it was used to form two new Rifle Divisions, the 140th in Uman' (from the 170th Rifle Regiment and the 146th (from the 198th Rifle Regiment) in Vinnitsa. What remained formed a new 58th Rifle Division.

Active Dates for the Great Patriotic War

None

Division Commanders

Unknown

Honors and Awards

None

Division Honorific Title

58th Rifle Division

Divisional Units

Unknown

Assignments during the Great Patriotic War

None

58th Rifle Division (III)

3rd Formation

The Division was formed in August 1939 in the Kiev Military District from what remained of the original 58th Rifle Division. It was transferred north to take part in the war with Finland in late 1939. In December 1939, it was ordered to reorganize into a Motorized Rifle Division, which it began to in January 1940.

Active Dates for the Great Patriotic War

None

Division Commanders

Unknown

Honors and Awards

None

Division Honorific Title

58th Rifle Division

Divisional Units (21.8.1939)

170th Rifle Regiment
279th Rifle Regiment
335th Rifle Regiment (disbanded in.1.1940)
244th Artillery Regiment (formerly the 58th Artillery Regiment)
258th Howitzer Artillery Regiment
81st Separate Reconnaissance Battalion
138th Separate Anti-Tank Battalion
151st Separate Anti-Aircraft Artillery Battalion (renamed the 125th Separate AAA Battalion)
126th Separate Sapper Battalion
100th Separate Signals Battalion

Assignments during the Great Patriotic War

None

58th Rifle Division (IV)

4th Formation

The Division was formed in April 1940 in the Kiev Special Military District when the 58th Motorized Division was ordered to reorganize back to a Rifle Division. It was a unique organization at the time. Although ordered to form as a "12,000" man Division, it was only authorized to have 2 Rifle Regiments and one Artillery Regiment. It remained in the Kiev Special Military District until May 1941 when it was reorganized again, this time to a Mountain Rifle Division.

Active Dates for the Great Patriotic War

None

Division Commanders

Unknown

Honors and Awards

None

Division Honorific Title

58th Rifle Division

Divisional Units

170th Rifle Regiment
279th Rifle Regiment
244th Artillery Regiment

Assignments during the Great Patriotic War

None

58th Rifle Division (V)

5th Formation

The Division was formed on 25 December 1941 by renaming the 431st Rifle Division in the Volga Military District. It spent the first four months of 1942 in the Military District and STAVKA Reserves training. It was then assigned to 50th Army in the Western Front in a relatively quite sector of the front. The Division was transferred to 49th Army in April of 1943. In August 1943 the Division participated in the Smolensk Offensive Operation advancing toward Mogilev. At the end of the year it was sent back to STAVKA Reserves to rest and refit. In January 1944, it was assigned to 40th Army of the 1st Ukrainian Front and took part in the Korsun-Shevchenkovsky Operation, suffering heavily as the Army took the brunt of the German relief attempt. Back in STAVKA Reserves to rebuild from February to April, the Division was assigned to 3rd Guards Army which it spent the rest of the war with. On 13 July it participated in the L'vov-Sandomierz Offensive which pushed the Germans back into Poland and established a bridgehead over the Vistula. From that bridgehead, the division participated in the Vistula-Oder Offensive where it fought its way to the Oder River north of Breslau. The Division then participated in the Berlin Offensive in April 1945, and finally the Prague Offensive in May 1945. The Division ended the war west of Prague on the line-of-contact with the Allied forces near Plzen. The Division became part of the Central Group of Forces occupying Czechoslovakia. As part of this Group, the Division was ordered to disband in June 1945, by STAVKA Order No. 11096 (CFG), dated 29 May 1945 and was disbanded shortly thereafter.

Active Dates for the Great Patriotic War

7 April 1942 - 25 November 1943
1 January 1944 - 24 February 1944
18 April 1944 - 11 May 1945

Division Commanders

25.12.1941 - 10.11.1942	Colonel Nikolai Nikolaevich SHKODUNOVICH
11.11.1942 - 30.4.1945	Colonel Vasilii Akimovich SAMSONOV (promoted to General-Major on 13.9.1944)
1.5.1945 - 11.5.1945	Colonel Aleksandr Andreevich SHIKITA

Honors and Awards

9.8.1944	Awarded the Order of the Red Banner
5.4.1945	Awarded the Honorific designation "Oder"
4.6.1945	Awarded the Order of Kutuzov II class

Division Honorific Title

58th Oder Red Banner Order of Kutuzov Rifle Division

Divisional Units

170th Rifle Regiment
279th Rifle Regiment
335th Rifle Regiment
244th Artillery Regiment
138th Separate Antitank Artillery Battalion
126th Mortar Battalion (until 10.11.1942)
544th Reconnaissance Company
126th Sapper Battalion (formally 81st Sapper Battalion)
100th Separate Signals Battalion (formally 392nd Separate Signals Company)
114th Medical Battalion
528th Separate Chemical Defense Company
132nd Auto-Transport Company
444th Field Bakery
909th Veterinary Field Hospital
1657th Field Postal Station
1086th Field Cash Office of the State Bank

Operations

Smolensk Strategic Offensive Operation	
Spas-Demensk Army Group Offensive Operation	7.8.1943 - 20.8.1943
Yelnia-Dorogobuzh Army Group Offensive Operation	28.8.1943 - 6.9.1943
Smolensk-Roslavl' Army Group Offensive Operation	15.9.1943 - 2.10.1943
Dnepr-Carpathian Strategic Offensive Operation	
Korsun-Shevchenkovsky Army Group Offensive Operation	24.1.1944 - 17.2.1944
L'vov-Sandomierz Strategic Offensive Operation	
Stanislav Army Group Offensive Operation	13.7.1944 - 27.7.1944
Vistula-Oder Strategic Offensive Operation	
Sandomierz-Silesian Army Group Offensive Operation	12.1.1945 - 3.2.1945
Lower Silesian Army Group Offensive Operation	8.2.1945 - 24.2.1945
Berlin Strategic Offensive Operation	
Cottbus-Potsdam Army Group Offensive Operation	16.4.1945 - 5.5.1945
Prague Strategic Offensive Operation	
Dresden-Prague Army Group Offensive Operation	6.5.1945 - 11.5.1945

Assignments during the Great Patriotic War

Date	Front	Army	Corps
1 January 1942	Volga Military District	-	-
1 February 1942	Volga Military District	-	-
1 March 1942	STAVKA Reserves	-	-
1 April 1942	STAVKA Reserves	-	-
1 May 1942	Western Front	50th Army	-
1 June 1942	Western Front	50th Army	-
1 July 1942	Western Front	50th Army	-
1 August 1942	Western Front	50th Army	-
1 September 1942	Western Front	50th Army	-
1 October 1942	Western Front	50th Army	-
1 November 1942	Western Front	50th Army	-
1 December 1942	Western Front	50th Army	-
1943			
1 January 1943	Western Front	50th Army	-
1 February 1943	Western Front	50th Army	-
1 March 1943	Western Front	50th Army	-
1 April 1943	Western Front	50th Army	-
1 May 1943	Western Front	49th Army	-
1 June 1943	Western Front	49th Army	-
1 July 1943	Western Front	49th Army	-
1 August 1943	Western Front	49th Army	-
1 September 1943	Western Front	49th Army	-
1 October 1943	Western Front	33rd Army	65th Rifle Corps
1 November 1943	Western Front	31st Army	70th Rifle Corps
1 December 1943	STAVKA Reserves	20th Army	103rd Rifle Corps
1944			
1 January 1944	STAVKA Reserves	47th Army	106th Rifle Corps
1 February 1944	1st Ukrainian Front	40th Army	104th Rifle Corps
1 March 1944	STAVKA Reserves	3rd Guards Army	21st Rifle Corps
1 April 1944	STAVKA Reserves	3rd Guards Army	-
1 May 1944	1st Ukrainian Front	3rd Guards Army	-
1 June 1944	1st Ukrainian Front	3rd Guards Army	22nd Rifle Corps
1 July 1944	1st Ukrainian Front	3rd Guards Army	22nd Rifle Corps
August 1944	1st Ukrainian Front	3rd Guards Army	22nd Rifle Corps
1 September 1944	1st Ukrainian Front	3rd Guards Army	22nd Rifle Corps
1 October 1944	1st Ukrainian Front	3rd Guards Army	22nd Rifle Corps
1 November 1944	1st Ukrainian Front	3rd Guards Army	22nd Rifle Corps
1 December 1944	1st Ukrainian Front	3rd Guards Army	22nd Rifle Corps

Date	Front	Army	Corps
1945			
1 January 1945	1st Ukrainian Front	3rd Guards Army	21st Rifle Corps
1 February 1945	1st Ukrainian Front	3rd Guards Army	21st Rifle Corps
1 March 1945	1st Ukrainian Front	3rd Guards Army	21st Rifle Corps
1 April 1945	1st Ukrainian Front	3rd Guards Army	21st Rifle Corps
1 May 1945	1st Ukrainian Front	3rd Guards Army	21st Rifle Corps
1 June 1945	Central Group of Forces	3rd Guards Army	21st Rifle Corps

58th Rifle Division (VI)

6th Formation

There is new information that the Division was re-formed in 1955, by the renaming of the 344th Rifle Division. It was assigned to the Turkestan Military District, although to which Corps Headquarters it was assigned to remains unclear. Like all of the Divisions formed in 1955, it did not last long however. The Division, as part of the reorganization of the Soviet Army in 1957, became the 58th Motorized Rifle Division.

Division Commanders

Unknown

Honors and Awards

Division carried over awards from the 344th Rifle Division
None awarded during 1955-1957

Division Honorific Title

58th Roslavl' Red Banner Rifle Division

Divisional Units

Currently unknown, but probably same numbered Regiments as previous Division.

59th Rifle Division (I)

1st Formation

The Division was formed 25 May 1936 from the cadre of the special collective farm rifle divisions in the Coastal Region of Far Eastern Army. There it remained, keeping a close watch on the Japanese until 1945. With the orders to invaded Manchuria, the Division was part of the 1st Red Banner Army in the Harbin-Kirin Army Group Offensive Operation in August 1945. After the war, it returned to the USSR and was re-assigned to the 26th Rifle Corps of the 35th Army in the Coastal Military District. Shortly thereafter in later 1945, it was re-organized into the 2nd Mechanized Division.

Active Dates for the Great Patriotic War

9 August 1945 - 3 September 1945

Division Commanders

3.7.1939 – 23.6.1941	Brigade Commander Vasilii Afanas'evich GLAZUNOV (promoted to General-Major on 4.6.1940)
24.6.1941 – 8.7.1941	Unknown
9.7.1941 – 9.1.1942	Colonel Aleksei Romanovich GNECHKO (promoted to General-Major on 8.12.1941)
10.1.1942 – 25.6.1943	Colonel Ivan Zakharovich PASHKOV (promoted to General-Major on 7.12.1942)
26.6.1943 – 12.5.1944	Colonel Fedor Ivanovich SUIN
13.5.1944 – 30.5.1944	Unknown
31.5.1944 – 3.9.1945	Colonel Matvei Stepanovich BATRAKOV (promoted to General-Major on 20.4.1945)

Honors and Awards

19.9.1945	Awarded the Order of the Red Banner

Division Honorific Title

59th Red Banner Rifle Division

Divisional Units

5th Rifle Regiment (formerly the 174th Rifle Regiment)
99th Rifle Regiment (formerly the 176th Rifle Regiment)
124th Rifle Regiment (formerly the 177th Rifle Regiment)
37th Artillery Regiment
45th Howitzer Artillery Regiment[2] (until.1.1942)
101st Separate Antitank Artillery Battalion
456th Separate Antiaircraft Artillery Battalion
45th Reconnaissance Company (formally 45th Reconnaissance Battalion)
35th Sapper Battalion
8th Separate Signals Battalion
17th Medical Battalion
49th Separate Chemical Defense Company
352nd Auto-Transport Company
28th Field Bakery
27th Mobile Field Hospital
50th Divisional Artillery Workshop
211th Veterinary Field Hospital
397th Field Postal Station
241st Field Cash Office of the State Bank

Operations

Manchurian Strategic Offensive Operation
Sungari Army Group Offensive Operation 9.8.1945 – 3.9.1945

Assignments during the Great Patriotic War

Date	Front	Army	Corps
January – December 1941	Far Eastern Front	1st Red Banner Army	59th Rifle Corps (June – Sept)
January – December 1942	Far Eastern Front	1st Red Banner Army	26th Rifle Corps
January – December 1943	Far Eastern Front	1st Red Banner Army	26th Rifle Corps
January – December 1944	Far Eastern Front	1st Red Banner Army	26th Rifle Corps
January – 1 August 1945	Far Eastern Front	1st Red Banner Army	26th Rifle Corps
8 August 1945	1st Far Eastern Front	1st Red Banner Army	-
3 September 1945	1st Far Eastern Front	1st Red Banner Army	-

---

[2] The 45th was initially formed on 1 September 1938 as the 59th Artillery Regiment. It was renumbered to the 45th Howitzer on 27 September 1939, when it is probable the 37th Artillery was formed.

59th Rifle Division (II)

2nd Formation

There is new information that the Division was re-formed in 1955, by the renaming of the 358th Rifle Division. It was assigned to the Far East Military District, initially as part of the 39th Army, then later as part of the 5th Army. Like all of the Divisions formed in 1955, it did not last long however. The Division, as part of the reorganization of the Soviet Army in 1957, became the 138th Motorized Rifle Division.

Division Commanders

Unknown

Honors and Awards

Division carried over awards from the 358th Rifle Division
None awarded during 1955-1957

Division Honorific Title

59th Leningrad-Khigan Red Banner Order of Suvorov Rifle Division

Divisional Units

Currently unknown, but probably same numbered Regiments as previous Division.

60th Rifle Division (I)

1st Formation

The Division was formed in July 1936 from the 1st Caucasian Rifle Division in the Ukrainian (later Kiev Special) Military District. During September 1939 it participated in the invasion of Poland as part of the 15th Rifle Corps, 5th Army. The Division also took part in the Soviet-Finish War in late 1939 and early 1940, sustaining heavy losses. After the war, it was transferred south to the Ukraine as part of the forces to invade Bessarabia. On 24 April 1941, the Division was reorganized as a Mountain Rifle Division.

Active Dates for the Great Patriotic War

None

Division Commanders

Unknown

Honors and Awards

1936	Awarded the Order of the Red Banner
1936	Awarded the honorific designation "in the name of Stepin"

Division Honorific Title

60th Caucasian Rifle Division in the name of Stepin

Divisional Units (21.8.1939)

194th Rifle Regiment (formerly 178th Rifle Regiment)
283rd Rifle Regiment (formerly 179th Rifle Regiment)
358th Rifle Regiment (formerly 180th Rifle Regiment)
54th Artillery Regiment
83rd Howitzer Artillery Regiment
52nd Separate Reconnaissance Battalion
33rd Separate Anti-Aircraft Artillery Battalion
71st Separate Anti-Tank Battalion
76th Separate Sapper Battalion
83rd Separate Signals Battalion

Assignments during the Great Patriotic War

None

60th Rifle Division (II)

2nd Formation

The Division was formed on 26 September 1941 from the 1st Moscow Rifle Division of the People's Militia in 33rd Army of Reserve Front. The Division was immediately caught up in the defense of Moscow and shifted to 49th Army. It then participated in the counteroffensive north of Tula. In January, it was transferred south to Bryansk Front and remained there with 3rd Army until February of 1943. The Division was then transferred to Central Front and was defending in the Western side of the Kursk salient during the Battle of Kursk. In October 1943, it participated in the Byelorussian Strategic Offensive Operation, pushing the Germans back to the Dnepr in the area just south of Gomel. By this time (20.10.43), the Central Front had been renamed Byelorussian Front. The Division also won its honorific for the liberation of Sevsk. In January 1944, it participated in the Kalinkovichi-Mozyr Army Group Operation, establishing a bridgehead over the Dnepr for future offensives. In February, the Division was transferred to 47th Army, 2nd Byelorussian Front, and in July, it took part in the Lublin-Brest Army Group Operation, advancing on Warsaw. In January 1945, now in the 1st Byelorussian Front, the Division participated in the Vistula-Oder Strategic Offensive Operation, advancing toward Schneidemuhl and took part in the later stages of the East Pomeranian Offensive, attacking toward Stettin. The 47th Army was then moved south for the final offensive toward Berlin. The 47th Army attacked over the Oder River and swung around to the western side of Berlin and advanced to the Elbe River. The Division ended the war with 47th Army, on the line-of-contact with the Allied forces just east of Stendal. 47th Army became part of the Group of Soviet Occupation forces in Germany. The Army was relieved by 3rd Shock Army and the Division was returned to the USSR in late 1946 where it was reorganized into the 65th Mechanized Division.

Active Dates for the Great Patriotic War

26 September 1941 – 3 January 1942
1 February 1942 – 9 February 1944
5 March 1944 – 9 May 1945

Division Commanders

16.10.1941 – 13.11.1941	Colonel Vasilii Ivanovich KALININ
14.11.1941 – 7.11.1942	Colonel Mikhail Arsent'evich ZASHIBALOV
8.11.1942 – 27.8.1943	Colonel Ignatii Vikent'evich KLYARO (promoted to General-Major on 31.3.1943)

29.8.1943 – 25.3.1944	Colonel Aleksandr Viktorovich BOGOYAVLENSKII
26.3.1944 – 28.3.1944	Unknown
29.3.1944 – 14.3.1945	General-Major Viktor Georgievich CHERNOV
15.3.1945 – 9.5.1945	Colonel Georgii Stepanovich IVANOV

Honors and Awards

31.8.1943	Awarded the Honorific designation "Sevsk"
23.7.1944	Awarded the Order of the Red Banner
12.8.1944	Awarded the Order of Suvorov II class
19.2.1945	Awarded the Honorific designation "Warsaw"

Division Honorific Title

60th Sevsk Warsaw Red Banner Order of Suvorov Rifle Division

Divisional Units

1281st Rifle Regiment
1283rd Rifle Regiment
1285th Rifle Regiment
969th Artillery Regiment
71st Separate Antitank Artillery Battalion
468th Reconnaissance Company
696th Sapper Battalion (formally 84th Sapper Battalion)
857th Separate Signals Battalion
491st Medical Battalion
330th Separate Chemical Defense Company
327th Auto-Transport Company
260th Field Bakery
180th Veterinary Field Hospital
968th Field Postal Station
27th Field Cash Office of the State Bank

Operations

Moscow Strategic Defensive Operation	
Vyaz'ma Army Group Defensive Operation	2.10.1941 – 13.10.1941
Tula Army Group Defensive Operation	24.10.1941 – 5.12.1941
Moscow Strategic Offensive Operation	
Tula Army Group Offensive Operation	6.12.1941 – 16.12.1941
Kaluga Army Group Offensive Operation	17.12.1941 – 5.1.1942
Naro-Fominsk Army Group Offensive Operation	24.12.1941 – 8.1.1942
Rzhev-Vyaz'ma Strategic Offensive Operation	
Mozhaisk-Vyaz'ma Army Group Offensive Operation	10.1.1942 – 28.2.1942
Chernigov-Poltava Strategic Offensive Operation	
Chernigov-Pripyet Army Group Offensive Operation	26.8.1943 – 30.9.1943
Byelorussian Strategic Offensive Operation	

Gomel'sko-Rechitskaia Army Group Offensive Operation	30.9.1943 – 30.10.1943
Gomel'sko-Rechitskaia Army Group Offensive Operation	10.11.1943 – 30.11.1943
Kalinkovichi Army Group Offensive Operation	8.12.1943 – 11.12.1943
Kalinkovichi Army Group Offensive Operation	20.12.1943 – 27.12.1943
Kalinkovichi-Mozyr Army Group Operation	8.1.1944 – 26.2.1944
Byelorussian Strategic Offensive Operation	
Lublin-Brest Army Group Offensive Operation	18.7.1944 – 2.8.1944
Vistula-Oder Strategic Offensive Operation	
Warsaw-Poznan Army Group Offensive Operation	14.1.1945 – 3.2.1945
East Pomeranian Strategic Offensive Operation	
Arnswalde-Kolberg Army Group Offensive Operation	1.3.1945 – 18.3.1945
Altdamm Army Group Offensive Operation	18.3.1945 – 4.4.1945
Berlin Strategic Offensive Operation	
Brandenberg-Ratenow Army Group Offensive Operation	3.5.1945 – 8.5.1945

Assignments during the Great Patriotic War

Date	Front	Army	Corps
1 October 1941	Reserve Front	33rd Army	-
1 November 1941	Western Front	49th Army	-
1 December 1941	Western Front	49th Army	-
1942			
1 January 1942	Western Front	49th Army	-
1 February 1942	Bryansk Front	Front Reserves	-
1 March 1942	Bryansk Front	3rd Army	-
1 April 1942	Bryansk Front	3rd Army	-
1 May 1942	Bryansk Front	61st Army	-
1 June 1942	Bryansk Front	61st Army	-
1 July 1942	Bryansk Front	3rd Army	-
1 August 1942	Bryansk Front	3rd Army	-
1 September 1942	Bryansk Front	3rd Army	-
1 October 1942	Bryansk Front	3rd Army	-
1 November 1942	Bryansk Front	3rd Army	-
1 December 1942	Bryansk Front	3rd Army	-
1943			
1 January 1943	Bryansk Front	3rd Army	-
1 February 1943	Bryansk Front	3rd Army	-
1 March 1943	Central Front	2nd Tank Army	-
1 April 1943	Central Front	65th Army	-

Date	Front	Army	Corps
1 May 1943	Central Front	65th Army	-
1 June 1943	Central Front	65th Army	-
1 July 1943	Central Front	65th Army	27th Rifle Corps
1 August 1943	Central Front	65th Army	27th Rifle Corps
1 September 1943	Central Front	65th Army	27th Rifle Corps
1 October 1943	Central Front	65th Army	18th Rifle Corps
1 November 1943	Byelorussian Front	65th Army	18th Rifle Corps
1 December 1943	Byelorussian Front	65th Army	27th Rifle Corps
1944			
1 January 1944	Byelorussian Front	65th Army	27th Rifle Corps
1 February 1944	Byelorussian Front	65th Army	27th Rifle Corps
1 March 1944	2nd Byelorussian Front	47th Army	125th Rifle Corps
1 April 1944	2nd Byelorussian Front	47th Army	125th Rifle Corps
1 May 1944	1st Byelorussian Front	47th Army	125th Rifle Corps
1 June 1944	1st Byelorussian Front	47th Army	125th Rifle Corps
1 July 1944	1st Byelorussian Front	47th Army	125th Rifle Corps
1 August 1944	1st Byelorussian Front	47th Army	-
1 September 1944	1st Byelorussian Front	47th Army	77th Rifle Corps
1 October 1944	1st Byelorussian Front	47th Army	125th Rifle Corps
1 November 1944	1st Byelorussian Front	47th Army	125th Rifle Corps
1 December 1944	1st Byelorussian Front	47th Army	125th Rifle Corps
1945			
1 January 1945	1st Byelorussian Front	47th Army	125th Rifle Corps
1 February 1945	1st Byelorussian Front	47th Army	125th Rifle Corps
1 March 1945	1st Byelorussian Front	47th Army	125th Rifle Corps
1 April 1945	1st Byelorussian Front	47th Army	125th Rifle Corps
1 May 1945	1st Byelorussian Front	47th Army	125th Rifle Corps
1 June 1945	Group of Soviet Occupation Forces in Germany	47th Army	125th Rifle Corps

60th Rifle Division (III)

3rd Formation

There is new information that the Division was re-formed in 1955, by the renaming of the 349th Rifle Division. It was assigned to the 7th Guards Army in the Trans-Caucasus Military District. Like all of the Divisions formed in 1955, it did not last long however. The Division, as part of the reorganization of the Soviet Army in 1957, became the 139th Motorized Rifle Division.

Division Commanders

Unknown

Honors and Awards

Division carried over awards from the 349th Rifle Division
None awarded during 1955-1957

Division Honorific Title

60th Rifle Division

Divisional Units

Currently unknown, but probably same numbered Regiments as previous Division.

61st Rifle Division (I)

1st Formation

The Division was formed in the early 1930s in the Volga Military District. Very little is known about the Division before 1941 except for two things: first, that the Division Commander from 1933 to 1936 was the future Marshal of the Soviet Union F. I. Golikov and second, that in the beginning of 1941, it was at the "6" manning level, which means that is was virtually at cadre strength with an authorized strength of 5,900 personnel. On 22 June 1941 the Division was part of 21st Army in STAVKA Reserves en route from Penza to Chernigov. In early July 21st Army was transferred to Western Front and sent to the front to defend along the Dnepr River in the area of Rogachev. When Guderian turned his 2nd Panzergruppe south toward Kiev, the Division was caught in the resulting encirclement and destroyed. It was removed from the order of battle in August but not officially disbanded until 19 December 1941.

Active Dates for the Great Patriotic War

2 July 1941 - 19 September 1941

Division Commanders

23.8.1939 - 1.7.1941	Colonel Nikolai Andreevich PRISCHEPA
2.7.1941 - 15.8.1941	Colonel Aleksandr Emil'evich GOFMAN

Honors and Awards

None

Division Honorific Title

61st Rifle Division

Divisional Units

66th Rifle Regiment (I) (formally 181st Rifle Regiment)
221st Rifle Regiment (I) (formally 182nd Rifle Regiment)
307th Rifle Regiment (I) (formally 183rd Rifle Regiment)
55th Artillery Regiment (formally 61st Art Regt)
66th Howitzer Artillery Regiment

131st Separate Antitank Artillery Battalion
237th Separate Antiaircraft Artillery Battalion
99th Reconnaissance Battalion
112th Sapper Battalion
107th Separate Signals Battalion
22nd Medical Battalion
53rd Separate Chemical Defense Company
60th Auto-Transport Battalion (formally 88th Auto-Transport Company)
57th Field Bakery
123rd Field Postal Station
435th Field Cash Office of the State Bank

Operations

Battle of Smolensk

Smolensk Army Group Defensive Operation	10.7.1941 – 10.8.1941
Rogechev-Zhlobin Army Group Offensive Operation	13.7.1941 – 24.7.1941

Kiev Strategic Defensive Operation

Kiev-Priluki Army Group Defensive Operation	20.8.1941 – 26.9.1941

Assignments during the Great Patriotic War

Date	Front	Army	Corps
22 June 1941	STAVKA Reserve	21st Army	66th Rifle Corps
1 July 1941	STAVKA Reserve	21st Army	63rd Rifle Corps
10 July 1941	Western Front	21st Army	63rd Rifle Corps
1 August 1941	Central front	21st Army	63rd Rifle Corps

61st Rifle Division (II)

2nd Formation

The Division was formed at the end of October 1941 in Yerevan, Armenia in the Trans-Caucasian Front. In December of 1941, it was assigned to 45th Army which was an inactive Army defending along the border with Turkey. In August 1942, with the Germans advancing toward the Caucasus oil fields, the Division was transferred to the Front and assigned to 46th Army and defended the mountain passes along the Black Sea Coast. In January 1943, it participated in the offensive that drove the Germans from the Caucasus region and back toward the Taman peninsula. Now with 56th Army, it took part in the Taman Army Group offensive which liberated Krasnodar. It was awarded the Order of the Red Banner for its combat activities during these battles. In August, the Division was transferred to Southern Front and placed in the 44th Army. It participated in the Lower Dnepr Strategic Offensive Operation, and in 1944, the Nikopol' Krivoi-Rog Operation helping in the liberation of Nikopol' and winning its honorific designation. After a short stay in STAVKA Reserves to rebuild, the Division was now assigned to 28th Army and placed in the 1st Byelorussian Front. During the Byelorussian Offensive, the Division fought its way to the outskirts of Warsaw. Again in September 1944, 28th Army was sent to rebuild in STAVKA Reserves and then transferred to the 3rd Byelorussian Front in late October. In January 1945, it participated in the East Prussian Strategic Offensive Operation, advancing to Königsberg. After clearing East Prussia, the Division, along with 28th Army, was sent south to 1st Ukrainian Front to participate in the final offensive to capture Prague. It ended the war in Czechoslovakia, northeast of Prague near Mlada-Voleslav. After the war, it was not one of the Divisions slated for occupation duty in Czechoslovakia, but was returned to the USSR and assigned to the Baranovichi Military District, still as part of the 128th Rifle Corps of the 28th Army. It was probably disbanded sometime in 1946.

Active Dates for the Great Patriotic War

20 August 1942 - 29 March 1944
28 May 1944 - 14 September 1944
13 October 1944 - 31 March 1945
20 April 1945 - 11 May 1945

Division Commanders

18.10.1941 - 15.2.1944 Colonel Sergei Nikolaevich KUZNETSOV (promoted to General-Major on 31.3.1943)

16.2.1944 - 1.3.1944	Colonel Aleksandr Nikolaevich BURYKIN
2.3.1944 - 11.5.1945	Colonel Andrei Georgievich SHATSKOV (promoted to General-Major on 5.5.1945)

Honors and Awards

28.4.1943	Awarded the Order of the Red Banner
13.2.1944	Awarded the Honorific designation "Nikopol'"
10.8.1944	Awarded the Order of Suvorov II class
24.4.1945	Awarded the Order of Lenin

Division Honorific Title

61st Nikopol' Red Banner Orders of Suvorov and Lenin Rifle Division

Divisional Units

66th Rifle Regiment (II)
221st Rifle Regiment (II) Awarded the Honorific designation "Berlin"
307th Rifle Regiment (II)
55th Artillery Regiment
237th Separate Antitank Artillery Battalion (until 15.7.1943)
131st Separate Antitank Artillery Battalion (from 15.7.1943)
172nd Separate Antiaircraft Artillery Battery (until 31.5.1943)
467th Mortar Battalion (until 26.8.1942)
99th Reconnaissance Company
112th Sapper Battalion
107th Separate Signals Battalion (formally 786th Sep. Signals Company)
22nd Medical Battalion
53rd Separate Chemical Defense Company
88th Auto-Transport Company
22nd Field Bakery
207th Veterinary Field Hospital
1723rd Field Postal Station
435th Field Cash Office of the State Bank

Operations

North Caucasus Strategic Defensive Operation	
Novorossiysk Army Group Defensive Operation	19.8.1942 - 26.9.1942
North Caucasus Strategic Offensive Operation	
Novorossiysk-Maikop Army Group Offensive Operation	11.1.1943 - 4.2.1943
Krasnodar Army Group Offensive Operation	9.2.1943 - 25.3.1943
Taman Army Group Offensive	4.4.1943 - 10.5.1943
Taman Army Group Offensive	26.5.1943 - 22.8.1943
Donbass Strategic Offensive Operation	
Mius-Mariupol' Army Group Offensive Operation	18.8.1943 - 22.9.1943
Lower Dnepr Strategic Offensive Operation	
Melitpol Army Group Offensive Operation	26.9.1943 - 5.11.1943

Nikopol' Army Group Offensive Operation	14.11.1943 - 31.12.1943
Nikopol'-Krivoi Rog Army Group Offensive Operation	30.1.1944 - 29.2.1944
Byelorussian Strategic Offensive Operation	
Bobruisk Army Group Offensive Operation	24.6.1944 - 29.7.1944
Lublin-Brest Army Group Offensive Operation	18.7.1944 - 2.8.1944
Goldap Army Group Offensive Operation	16.10.1944 - 30.10.1944
East Prussian Strategic Offensive Operation	
Insterburg-Königsberg Army Group Offensive Operation	14.1.1945 - 26.1.1945
Rastenburg-Heilsberg Army Group Offensive Operation	27.1.1945 - 12.2.1945
Braunsburg Army Group Offensive Operation	13.3.1945 - 22.3.1945
Prague Strategic Offensive Operation	
Sudeten Army Group Offensive Operation	6.5.1945 - 11.5.1945

Assignments during the Great Patriotic War

Date	Front	Army	Corps
1 November 1941	Trans-Caucasian Front	Front Reserve	-
1 December 1941	Trans-Caucasian Front	Front Reserve	-
1943			
1 January 1942	Caucasian Front – Inactive Armies	45th Army	-
1 February 1942	Trans-Caucasian Military District	45th Army	-
1 March 1942	Trans-Caucasian Military District	45th Army	-
1 April 1942	Trans-Caucasian Military District	45th Army	-
1 May 1942	Trans-Caucasian Military District	45th Army	-
1 June 1942	Trans-Caucasian Front – Inactive Armies	45th Army	-
1 July 1942	Trans-Caucasian Front – Inactive Armies	45th Army	-
1 August 1942	Trans-Caucasian Front – Inactive Armies	45th Army	-
1 September 1942	Trans-Caucasian Front – Northern Group of Forces	46th Army	-
1 October 1942	Trans-Caucasian Front – Black Sea Group of Forces	46th Army	-

Date	Front	Army	Corps
1 November 1942	Trans-Caucasian Front – Black Sea Group of Forces	46th Army	-
1 December 1942	Trans-Caucasian Front – Northern Group of Forces	46th Army	-
1943			
1 January 1943	Trans-Caucasian Front – Black Sea Group of Forces	46th Army	-
1 February 1943	Trans-Caucasian Front – Black Sea Group of Forces	56th Army	-
1 March 1943	North Caucasian Front – Black Sea Group of Forces	56th Army	-
1 April 1943	North Caucasian Front	56th Army	-
1 May 1943	North Caucasian Front	56th Army	-
1 June 1943	North Caucasian Front	56th Army	
1 July 1943	North Caucasian Front	Front Reserve	16th Rifle Corps
1 August 1943	North Caucasian Front	56th Army	16th Rifle Corps
1 September 1943	Southern Front	Front Reserve	-
1 October 1943	Southern Front	44th Army	63rd Rifle Corps
1 November 1943	4th Ukrainian Front	44th Army	63rd Rifle Corps
1 December 1943	4th Ukrainian Front	28th Army	9th Rifle Corps
1944			
1 January 1944	4th Ukrainian Front	28th Army	10th Guards Rifle Corps
1 February 1944	4th Ukrainian Front	Front Reserve	-
1 March 1944	3rd Ukrainian Front	5th Shock Army	37th Rifle Corps
1 April 1944	STAVKA Reserves	28th Army	-
1 May 1944	STAVKA Reserves	28th Army	128th Rifle Corps
1 June 1944	1st Byelorussian Front	28th Army	128th Rifle Corps
1 July 1944	1st Byelorussian Front	28th Army	128th Rifle Corps
1 August 1944	1st Byelorussian Front	28th Army	128th Rifle Corps
1 September 1944	1st Byelorussian Front	28th Army	128th Rifle Corps
1 October 1944	STAVKA Reserves	28th Army	128th Rifle Corps
1 November 1944	3rd Byelorussian Front	28th Army	128th Rifle Corps
1 December 1944	3rd Byelorussian Front	28th Army	128th Rifle Corps
1945			
1 January 1945	3rd Byelorussian Front	28th Army	128th Rifle Corps
1 February 1945	3rd Byelorussian Front	28th Army	128th Rifle Corps

Date	Front	Army	Corps
1 March 1945	3rd Byelorussian Front	28th Army	128th Rifle Corps
1 April 1945	STAVKA Reserves	28th Army	128th Rifle Corps
1 May 1945	1st Ukrainian Front	28th Army	128th Rifle Corps

61st Rifle Division (III)

3rd Formation

There is new information that the Division was re-formed in 1955, by the renaming of the 357th Rifle Division. It was assigned to the Turkestan Military District, although to which Corps headquarters remains unclear. Like all of the Divisions formed in 1955, it did not last long however. The Division, as part of the reorganization of the Soviet Army in 1957, became the 61st Motorized Rifle Division.

Division Commanders

Unknown

Honors and Awards

Division carried over awards from the 357th Rifle Division
None awarded during 1955-1957

Division Honorific Title

61st Order of Suvorov Rifle Division

Divisional Units

Currently unknown, but probably same numbered Regiments as previous Division.

62nd Rifle Division (I)

1st Formation

The Division was formed in July 1936 from the 2nd Turkestan Rifle Division. It took part in the invasion of Bessarabia in June 1940 as part of the 13th Rifle Corps, 12th Army. On 22 June 1941 it was stationed in 5th Army in Lutsk in the Kiev Special Military District which became Southwestern Front. The Division fought in the defensive battles with 5th Army around Kiev and was trapped in the encirclement in September. The Division was destroyed and removed from the order of battle on 19 September 1941.

Active Dates for the Great Patriotic War

22 June 1941 - 19 September 1941

Division Commanders

9.10.1940 - 19.9.1941	Colonel Mikhail Pavlovich TIMOSHENKO

Honors and Awards

None

Division Honorific Title

62nd Turkestan Rifle Division

Divisional Units

104th Rifle Regiment (I) (formally 184th Rifle Regiment)(originally designated the 54th Rifle Regiment)
123rd Rifle Regiment (I) (formally 185th Rifle Regiment)
306th Rifle Regiment (I) (formally 186th Rifle Regiment)
89th Artillery Regiment (formally 62nd Artillery Regiment)
150th Howitzer Artillery Regiment
126th Separate Antitank Artillery Battalion
392nd Separate Antiaircraft Artillery Battalion (originally the 309th Separate AAA Battalion)
95th Separate Reconnaissance Battalion
108th Sapper Battalion (originally the 109th Separate Sapper Battalion)

93rd Separate Signals Battalion
33rd Medical Battalion
113th Separate Chemical Defense Company
56th Auto-Transport Battalion
72nd Mobile Field Bakery
399th Field Cash Office of the State Bank

Operations

L'vov-Chernovitsy Strategic Defensive Operation	
Border Defensive Battles	22.6.1941 – 27.6.1941
L'vov-Lutsk Army Group Defensive Operation	27.7.1941 – 2.7.1941
Kiev Strategic Defensive Operation	
Korosten' Army Group Defensive Operation	11.7.1941 – 20.8.1941
Kiev-Priluki Army Group Defensive Operation	20.8.1941 – 26.9.1941

Assignments during the Great Patriotic War

Date	Front	Army	Corps
22 June 1941	Southwestern Front	5th Army	15th Rifle Corps
1 July 1941	Southwestern Front	5th Army	15th Rifle Corps
10 July 1941	Southwestern Front	5th Army	15th Rifle Corps
1 August 1941	Southwestern Front	5th Army	15th Rifle Corps
September 1941	Southwestern Front	5th Army	15th Rifle Corps

62nd Rifle Division (II)

2nd Formation

The Division started forming in October of 1941 in the Khar'kov Military District. It was rushed to the front in November 1941 to form a new line of resistance east of Khar'kov after the destruction of the Kiev pocket. The Division was assigned to 40th Army when it arrived at the front. In July 1942, during the opening thrust of the German summer offensive "Plan Blue" the Division suffered heavy casualties and was withdrawn to the Volga Military District to rebuild. It was later transferred to 10th Reserve Army and was sent back to the front in late October as part of 66th Army in the newly formed Don Front. The Division took part in the counterattacks against the north flanks of the German thrust into Stalingrad and by early November, having suffered heavy casualties, it was disbanded and the remaining men were used to reinforce other divisions within 66th Army.

Active Dates for the Great Patriotic War

2 November 1941 - 29 July 1942
7 October 1942 - 21 November 1942

Division Commanders

25.11.1941 - 30.7.1942	Colonel Pavel Akimovich NAVROTSKII
1.8.1942 - 2.11.1942	Colonel Aleksei Stepanovich FROLOV

Honors and Awards

None

Division Honorific Title

62nd Rifle Division

Divisional Units

104th Rifle Regiment (II)
123rd Rifle Regiment (II)
306th Rifle Regiment (II)
89th Artillery Regiment
126th Separate Antitank Artillery Battalion

401st Separate Antiaircraft Artillery Battery (formally 392nd Separate Antiaircraft Artillery Battalion)
527th Mortar Battalion (from 18.11.1941)
6th Separate Machinegun Battalion
95th Reconnaissance Company
108th Sapper Battalion
93rd Separate Signals Battalion
33rd Medical Battalion
113th Separate Chemical Defense Company
56th Auto-Transport Company
72nd Field Bakery
771st Field Postal Station
1647th Field Cash Office of the State Bank (formally 547th Field Cash Office)

Operations

Oboyan-Kursk Army Group Offensive Operation	3.1.1942 – 26.1.1942
Voronezh-Voroshilovgrad Strategic Defensive Operation	
Kastornoye Army Group Defensive Operation	28.6.1942 – 10.7.1942
Stalingrad Strategic Defensive Operation	
Defensive Battles on the near approaches	19.8.1942 – 18.11.1942

Assignments during the Great Patriotic War

Date	Front	Army	Corps
1 December 1941	Southwestern Front	40th Army	-
1942			
1 January 1942	Southwestern Front	40th Army	-
1 February 1942	Southwestern Front	40th Army	-
1 March 1942	Southwestern Front	40th Army	-
1 April 1942	Southwestern Front	40th Army	-
1 May 1942	Bryansk Front	40th Army	-
1 June 1942	Bryansk Front	40th Army	-
1 July 1942	Bryansk Front	40th Army	-
1 August 1942	Volga Military District	-	-
1 September 1942	STAVKA Reserves	10th Reserve Army	-
1 October 1942	STAVKA Reserves	10th Reserve Army	-
1 November 1942	Don Front	66th Army	-

62nd Rifle Division (III)

3rd Formation

The Division was formed on 15 April 1943 from the cadre of the 44th Separate Rifle Brigade in the Moscow Military District. It was assigned to the 3rd Reserve Army in STAVKA Reserve to train. In July it was transferred to 21st Army in Western Front and during August/September participated in the Smolensk Strategic Offensive Operation, pushing the Germans back toward the Dnepr. In the fall of 1943, it took part in the Orsha Army Group Offensives. When Western Front became 3rd Byelorussian Front in April 1944, the Division was transferred to 31st Army and remained with that Army for the rest of the war. The Division next participated in the Byelorussian Operation, liberating Borisov and ended the offensive near Grodno. It won its honorific designation for the liberation Borisov, and the Order of the Red Banner for its actions throughout the offensive. In January 1945, the Division participated in the East Prussian Strategic Offensive advancing through Rastenburg and Königsberg. In April, 31st Army was transferred south to 1st Ukrainian Front for the final offensive to capture Prague. The Division ended the war northeast of Prague near Michik and became part of the Central Group of Forces occupying Czechoslovakia. As part of this Group, the Division was ordered to disband in June 1945, by STAVKA Order No. 11096 (CGF), dated 29 May 1945. Although unconfirmed, it is believed that it was not disbanded until June 1946.

Active Dates for the Great Patriotic War

12 July 1943 - 1 April 1945
21 April 1945 - 11 May 945

Division Commanders

15.4.1943 - 1.4.1944	General-Major Vasilii Vladimirovich YEFREMOV
2.4.1944 - 7.9.1944	General-Major Porfirii Grigor'evich BORODKIN
8.9.1944 - 9.5.1945	Colonel Semen Samuilovich LEVIN

Honors and Awards

10.3.1944	Awarded the Order of the Red Banner of Labor
10.6.1944	Awarded the Honorific designation "Borisov"
12.8.1944	Awarded the Order of the Red Banner
26.4.1945	Awarded the Order of Suvorov II class
19.5.1945	Awarded the Order of Kutuzov II Class

Division Honorific Title

62nd Borisov Red Banner Orders of Suvorov and Kutuzov Rifle Division

Divisional Units

104th Rifle Regiment (III)
123rd Rifle Regiment (III)
306th Rifle Regiment (III)
89th Artillery Regiment
126th Separate Antitank Artillery Battalion
95th Separate Reconnaissance Company
108th Sapper Battalion
424th Separate Signals Battalion (formally 393rd Separate Signals Company)
33rd Medical Battalion
113th Separate Chemical Defense Company
275th Auto-Transport Company
72nd Field Bakery
232nd Veterinary Field Hospital
1513th Field Postal Station
1647th Field Cash Office of the State Bank

Operations

Smolensk Strategic Offensive Operation	
Spas-Demensk Army Group Offensive Operation	7.8.1943 - 20.8.1943
Yelnia-Dorogobuzh Army Group Offensive Operation	28.8.1943 - 6.9.1943
Smolensk-Roslavl' Army Group Offensive Operation	15.9.1943 - 2.10.1943
Byelorussian Strategic Offensive Operation	
Orsha Army Group Offensive Operation	3.10.1943 - 26.10.1943
Orsha Army Group Offensive Operation	14.11.1943 - 5.12.1943
Byelorussian Strategic Offensive Operation	
Vitebsk Army Group Offensive Operation	23.6.1944 - 28.6.1944
Minsk Army Group Offensive Operation	29.6.1944 - 4.7.1944
Kaunas Army Group Offensive Operation	28.7.1944 - 28.8.1944
Goldap Army Group Offensive Operation	16.10.1944 - 30.10.1944
East Prussian Strategic Offensive Operation	
Insterburg-Königsberg Army Group Offensive Operation	14.1.1945 - 26.1.1945
Rastenburg-Heilsberg Army Group Offensive Operation	27.1.1945 - 12.2.1945
Braunsburg Army Group Offensive Operation	13.3.1945 - 22.3.1945
Prague Strategic Offensive Operation	
Sudenten Army Group Offensive Operation	6.5.1945 - 11.5.1945

Assignments during the Great Patriotic War

Date	Front	Army	Corps
1 May 1943	STAVKA Reserves	3rd Reserve Army	-
1 June 1943	STAVKA Reserves	3rd Reserve Army	-
1 July 1943	STAVKA Reserves	3rd Reserve Army	-
1 August 1943	Western Front	21st Army	61st Rifle Corps
1 September 1943	Western Front	21st Army	61st Rifle Corps
1 October 1943	Western Front	21st Army	61st Rifle Corps
1 November 1943	Western Front	33rd Army	61st Rifle Corps
1 December 1943	Western Front	33rd Army	61st Rifle Corps
1944			
1 January 1944	Western Front	49th Army	61st Rifle Corps
1 February 1944	Western Front	49th Army	61st Rifle Corps
1 March 1944	Western Front	49th Army	61st Rifle Corps
1 April 1944	Western Front	49th Army	-
1 May 1944	3rd Byelorussian Front	31st Army	113th Rifle Corps
1 June 1944	3rd Byelorussian Front	31st Army	113th Rifle Corps
1 July 1944	3rd Byelorussian Front	31st Army	113th Rifle Corps
1 August 1944	3rd Byelorussian Front	31st Army	113th Rifle Corps
1 September 1944	3rd Byelorussian Front	31st Army	71st Rifle Corps
1 October 1944	3rd Byelorussian Front	31st Army	71st Rifle Corps
1 November 1944	3rd Byelorussian Front	31st Army	36th Rifle Corps
1 December 1944	3rd Byelorussian Front	31st Army	71st Rifle Corps
1945			
1 January 1945	3rd Byelorussian Front	31st Army	-
1 February 1945	3rd Byelorussian Front	31st Army	44th Rifle Corps
1 March 1945	3rd Byelorussian Front	31st Army	44th Rifle Corps
1 April 1945	3rd Byelorussian Front	31st Army	44th Rifle Corps
1 May 1945	1st Ukrainian Front	31st Army	44th Rifle Corps
1 June 1945	Central Group of Forces	31st Army	44th Rifle Corps

62nd Rifle Division (IV)

4th Formation

There is new information that the Division was re-formed in 1955, by the renaming of the 360th Rifle Division. It was assigned to the 40th Army in the Turkestan Military District. Like all of the Divisions formed in 1955, it did not last long however. The Division, as part of the reorganization of the Soviet Army in 1957, became the 108th Motorized Rifle Division.

Division Commanders

Unknown

Honors and Awards

Division carried over awards from the 360th Rifle Division
None awarded during 1955-1957

Division Honorific Title

62nd Nevel Twice Red Banner Rifle Division

Divisional Units

Currently unknown, but probably same numbered Regiments as previous Division.

63rd Rifle Division (I)

1st Formation

The Division was formed in June/July 1942 in 21st Army of Southwestern Front, from cadre of the 8th NKVD Motorized Rifle Division. By August, the Southwestern Front became the first formation of Stalingrad Front, and the Division was defending along the Don River Bend. On 30 September 1942, Stalingrad Front became Don Front, and in late October the 21st Army was transferred to the new Southwestern Front in anticipation of the Stalingrad Offensive Operation. On 19 November 1942, Operation "Uranus" was launched and the Division helped in the crushing of the 3rd Rumanian Army. For recognition of its actions during this operation, the Division was awarded "Guards" status on 27 November 1942 and renamed 52nd Guards Rifle Division.

Active Dates for the Great Patriotic War

14 July 1942 - 27 November 1942

Division Commanders

25.6.1942 - 27.11.1942 Colonel Nester Dmitrievich KOZIN

Honors and Awards

None

Division Honorific Title

63rd Rifle Division

Divisional Units

units were awarded their "Guards" designation on 30.12.1942)

	Becomes
226th Rifle Regiment (I)	151st Guards Rifle Regiment
291st Rifle Regiment (I)	153rd Guards Rifle Regiment
346th Rifle Regiment (I)	155th Guards Rifle Regiment
26th Artillery Regiment (formally 10th Howitzer Artillery Regiment	124th Guards Artillery Regiment
273rd Separate Antitank Artillery Battalion	57th Guards Sep. AT Artillery Bn

109th Separate Antiaircraft Artillery Battery (formally 347 Sep. AA Artillery Battalion)	70th Guards Sep. AA Artillery Battery
175th Mortar Battalion (until 18.10.1942)	
53rd Reconnaissance Battalion	56th Guards Reconnaissance Co
170th Sapper Battalion	61st Guards Sapper Battalion
51st Separate Signals Battalion	82nd Guards Sep. Signals Battalion
116th Medical Battalion	562nd Medical Battalion
34th Separate Chemical Defense Company	58th Guards Chemical Defense Co
400th Auto-Transport Company	617th Auto-Transport Company
20th Field Bakery	640th Field Bakery
51st Veterinary Field Hospital	646th Veterinary Field Hospital
1593rd Field Postal Station	590th Field Postal Station
1013th Field Cash Office of the State Bank	1766th Field Cash Office of the State Bank

Operations

Stalingrad Strategic Defensive Operation	
Defensive Battles on the near approaches	19.8.1942 - 18.11.1942
Stalingrad Strategic Offensive Operation	
Operation Uranus	19.11.1942 - 30.11.1942

Assignments during the Great Patriotic War

Date	Front	Army	Corps
1 August 1942	Stalingrad Front	21st Army	-
1 September 1942	Stalingrad Front	21st Army	-
1 October 1942	Don Front	21st Army	-
1 November 1942	Southwestern Front	21st Army	-

63rd Rifle Division (II)

2nd Formation

The Division was formed on 18 April 1943 in the Moscow Military District, from cadre of the 45th and 86th Separate Rifle Brigades. The Division was placed in the 3rd Reserve Army in STAVKA Reserve for training until late July. At this time, it was assigned to 21st Army in Western Front and participated in the Smolensk Offensive Operation. In October 1943, the Division was transferred to 33rd Army and took part in the Orsha Army Group Offensives. After a transfer to 49th Army, for the first three months of 1944, and a transfer back to 33rd Army in late March, the Division was assigned to 5th Army when the Western Front became the 3rd Byelorussian Front. The Division remained with the 5th Army for the rest of the war. On 23 June, the Division participated in the Byelorussian Strategic Offensive, winning its honorific title and the Order of the Red Banner for its part in the liberation of Vitebsk. In September 1944, it took part in the Baltic Offensive Operation, pushing the Germans back toward East Prussia. For its actions during this offensive, the Division won the Order of Suvorov II class. On 3 January 1945, the Division participated in the East Prussian Offensive, battling the Germans back into Königsberg, and after its fall, the 5th Army went into STAVKA Reserves in order to refit and begin its travel to the Far East. Initially assigned to the Coastal Group of Forces near Vladivostok, at the start of the Manchurian Offensive the Army was assigned to 1st Far Eastern Front. For its actions during this offensive the Division won the Order of Kutuzov II class. After the war, the Division returned to the USSR later in 1945, still as part of the 72nd Rifle Corps, 5th Army, but now part of the Coastal Military District. It remained there until 1957 when it was reorganized into the 63rd Motorized Rifle Division.

Active Dates for the Great Patriotic War

12 July 1943 – 19 April 1945
9 August 1945 – 3 September 1945

Division Commanders

18.4.1943 – 8.2.1945	Colonel Nikolai Matveevich LASKIN (promoted to General-Major on 22.2.1944)
9.2.1945 – 16.2.1945	Colonel Nikolai Timofeevich ZORIN
17.2.1945 – 19.4.1945	General-Major Nikolai Matveevich LASKIN
20.4.1945 – 9.5.1945	Colonel Arsenii Ignat'evich GORDIENKO

Honors and Awards

2.7.1944	Awarded the Honorific designation "Vitebsk"
25.7.1944	Awarded the Order of the Red Banner
14.11.1944	Awarded the Order of Suvorov II class
9.9.1945	Awarded the Order of Kutuzov II class

Division Honorific Title

63rd Vitebsk Red Banner Orders of Suvorov and Kutuzov Rifle Division

Divisional Units

226th Rifle Regiment (II)
291st Rifle Regiment (II)
346th Rifle Regiment (II)
26th Artillery Regiment
273rd Separate Antitank Artillery Battalion
53rd Reconnaissance Company
170th Sapper Battalion
51st Separate Signals Battalion (formally 649th Sep. Signals Company)
116th Medical Battalion
34th Separate Chemical Defense Company
400th Auto-Transport Company
21st Field Bakery
51st Veterinary Field Hospital
1603rd Field Postal Station
78th Field Cash Office of the State Bank (formally 1648th Field Cash Office)

Operations

Smolensk Strategic Offensive Operation	
Spas-Demensk Army Group Offensive Operation	7.8.1943 - 20.8.1943
Yelnia-Dorogobuzh Army Group Offensive Operation	28.8.1943 - 6.9.1943
Smolensk-Roslavl' Army Group Offensive Operation	15.9.1943 - 2.10.1943
Byelorussian Strategic Offensive Operation	
Orsha Army Group Offensive Operation	3.10.1943 - 26.10.1943
Orsha Army Group Offensive Operation	14.11.1943 - 5.12.1943
Byelorussian Strategic Offensive Operation	
Vitebsk Army Group Offensive Operation	23.6.1944 - 28.6.1944
Minsk Army Group Offensive Operation	29.6.1944 - 4.7.1944
Kaunas Army Group Offensive Operation	28.7.1944 - 28.8.1944
Goldap Army Group Offensive Operation	16.10.1944 - 30.10.1944
East Prussian Strategic Offensive Operation	
Insterburg-Königsberg Army Group Offensive Operation	14.1.1945 - 26.1.1945
Rastenburg-Heilsberg Army Group Offensive Operation	27.1.1945 - 12.2.1945

Braunsburg Army Group Offensive Operation 13.3.1945 – 22.3.1945
Manchurian Strategic Offensive Operation
Sungari Army Group Offensive Operation 9.8.1945 – 2.9.1945

Assignments during the Great Patriotic War

Date	Front	Army	Corps
1 April 1943	Moscow Military District	-	-
1 May 1943	STAVKA Reserves	3rd Reserve Army	-
1 June 1943	STAVKA Reserves	3rd Reserve Army	-
1 July 1943	STAVKA Reserves	3rd Reserve Army	-
1 August 1943	Western Front	21st Army	-
1 September 1943	Western Front	21st Army	69th Rifle Corps
1 October 1943	Western Front	21st Army	-
1 November 1943	Western Front	33rd Army	61st Rifle Corps
1 December 1943	Western Front	33rd Army	61st Rifle Corps
1944			
1 January 1944	Western Front	49th Army	62nd Rifle Corps
1 February 1944	Western Front	49th Army	62nd Rifle Corps
1 March 1944	Western Front	49th Army	62nd Rifle Corps
1 April 1944	Western Front	33rd Army	62nd Rifle Corps
1 May 1944	3rd Byelorussian Front	5th Army	65th Rifle Corps
1 June 1944	3rd Byelorussian Front	5th Army	72nd Rifle Corps
1 July 1944	3rd Byelorussian Front	5th Army	72nd Rifle Corps
1 August 1944	3rd Byelorussian Front	5th Army	72nd Rifle Corps
1 September 1944	3rd Byelorussian Front	5th Army	72nd Rifle Corps
1 October 1944	3rd Byelorussian Front	5th Army	72nd Rifle Corps
1 November 1944	3rd Byelorussian Front	5th Army	72nd Rifle Corps
1 December 1944	3rd Byelorussian Front	5th Army	72nd Rifle Corps
1945			
1 January 1945	3rd Byelorussian Front	5th Army	72nd Rifle Corps
1 February 1945	3rd Byelorussian Front	5th Army	72nd Rifle Corps
1 March 1945	3rd Byelorussian Front	5th Army	72nd Rifle Corps
1 April 1945	3rd Byelorussian Front	5th Army	72nd Rifle Corps
1 May 1945	STAVKA Reserves	5th Army	72nd Rifle Corps
1 June 1945	Coastal Group of Forces	5th Army	72nd Rifle Corps
1 July 1945	Coastal Group of Forces	5th Army	72nd Rifle Corps
1 August 1945	Coastal Group of Forces	5th Army	72nd Rifle Corps
9 August 1945	1st Far Eastern Front	5th Army	72nd Rifle Corps

Date	Front	Army	Corps
3 September 1945	1st Far Eastern Front	5th Army	72nd Rifle Corps

64th Rifle Division (I)

1st Formation

There is conflicting information when the Division was formed. One source states it was 1923. Another it wasn't until the late 1920s. In either case, it was garrisoned in Smolensk in the Byelorussian Military District. Sometime in the later half of the 1930s, it was upgraded to a 'cadre' Division, but still remained in Smolensk. In August/September of 1939, as part of the partial mobilization conducted by the USSR, it was ordered to form two new Divisions, the 145th and 164th Rifle Divisions, each based around one of the Divisions Rifle Regiments. What remained formed a new 64th Rifle Division.

Active Dates for the Great Patriotic War

None

Division Commanders

Unknown

Honors and Awards

None

Division Honorific Title

64th Rifle Division

Divisional Units

190th Rifle Regiment
191st Rifle Regiment
192nd Rifle Regiment
64th Artillery Regiment

Assignments during the Great Patriotic War

None

64th Rifle Division (II)

2nd Formation

The Division was formed in September 1939 from what remained of the original 64th Rifle Division probably based around the 192nd Rifle Regiment. It was raised as a '6' Division, having an authorized strength of approximately 5,900 men. On 22 June the Division was assigned to Western Front Reserves with the 44th Rifle Corps. As the Germans pushed past Minsk in late June, the Division was rushed to the front to defend along the Dnepr River with 13th Army. After the Division was sent to Front Reserves, for most of July it was assigned to 19th Army and took part in the Yelnia Offensive. For recognition of its actions during this offensive, the Division was awarded "Guards" status on 26 September 1941 and renamed 7th Guards Rifle Division.

Active Dates for the Great Patriotic War

22 June 1941 - 19 September 1941

Division Commanders

1.6.1940 – 23.7.1941	Colonel Sergei Ivanovich IOVLEV
24.7.1941 - 26.9.1941	Colonel Afanasii Sergeevich GRYAZNOV

Honors and Awards

None

Division Honorific Title

64th Rifle Division

Divisional Units

units were awarded their "Guards" designation on 20.2.1942)

	Becomes
30th Rifle Regiment	14th Guards Rifle Regiment
159th Rifle Regiment	20th Guards Rifle Regiment
288th Rifle Regiment	26th Guards Rifle Regiment
163rd Artillery Regiment	25th Guards Artillery Regiment

219th Howitzer Artillery Regiment	
170th Separate Antitank Artillery Battalion	1st Guards Sep. AT Artillery Battalion
318th Separate Antiaircraft Artillery Battalion	
73rd Reconnaissance Battalion	4th Guards Reconnaissance Co
106th Sapper Battalion	12th Guards Sapper Battalion
82nd Separate Signals Battalion	6th Guards Sep. Signals Battalion
65th Medical Battalion	475th Medical Battalion
178th Auto-Transport Company	477th Auto-Transport Company
99th Field Bakery	605th Field Bakery
100th Veterinary Field Hospital	Veterinary Field Hospital
140th Field Postal Station	no change
105th Field Cash Office of the State Bank	no change

Operations

The Battle of Smolensk

Smolensk Army Group Defensive Operation	10.7.1941 - 10.8.1941
Dukhovshchina Army Group Offensive Operation	30.8.1941 - 8.9.1941

Assignments during the Great Patriotic War

Date	Front	Army	Corps
22 June 1941	Western Front	Front Reserves	44th Rifle Corps
1 July 1941	Western Front	13th Army	44th Rifle Corps
10 July 1941	Western Front	Front Reserves	44th Rifle Corps
1 August 1941	Western Front	Group of Forces Yartsevo Direction	44th Rifle Corps
1 September 1941	Western Front	19th Army	-

64th Rifle Division (III)

3rd Formation

The Division was formed during February and March of 1942 from the cadre of the 7th Sapper Brigade in the Moscow Military District. In late May, it was assigned to 8th Reserve Army in STAVKA Reserve. The Division was transferred to 1st Guards Army in Stalingrad Front in August to take part in the defensive operations along the Don Bend. Later in September, it was transferred to 66th Army, which was created from the 8th Reserve Army in Don Front, which itself was formed by renaming Stalingrad Front. The Division participated in the Stalingrad Offensive Operation and later Operation Kol'tso, which destroyed the German 6th Army. After Stalingrad, the Division went into STAVKA Reserve to refit and rebuild and then was sent north and assigned to 16th Army in Western Front. After a transfer to 50th Army, the Division was then assigned to 10th Army in early August to participate in the Smolensk Offensive. In February 1944, the 10th Army was transferred to 1st Byelorussian Front, and then in April the Division was transferred to 49th Army in 2nd Byelorussian Front. It participated in Byelorussian Operation "Bagration", winning its honorific and the Order of Suvorov II class for its actions during the offensive. After being refit in STAVKA Reserves for October, the Division was sent back to the Front with 33rd Army in 1st Byelorussian Front. It participated in the Vistula-Oder Offensive and then transferred to 3rd Shock Army to take part in the Berlin Offensive. As part of the Soviet Group of Occupation Forces in Germany, it was ordered to disband in June 1945 by STAVKA VGK Order No. 11095 (GSOFG) dated 29 May 1945; but was actually disbanded 31 October 1945.

Active Dates for the Great Patriotic War

25 August 1942 - 9 September 1944
19 October 1944 - 9 May 1945

Division Commanders

5.3.1942 - 1.6.1943	Colonel Aleksandr Mikhailovich IGNATOV
2.6.1943 - 12.6.1943	Unknown
13.6.1943 - 3.6.1944	Colonel Ivan Ivanovich YAREMENKO
4.6.1944 - 9.5.1945	General-Major Timofei Kalinovich SHKRYLEV

Honors and Awards

June 1944	Awarded the Honorific designation "Mogilev"
1.9.1944	warded the Order of Suvorov II class
11.6.1945	Awarded the Order of Kutuzov II class

Division Honorific Title

64th Mogilev Orders of Suvorov and Kutuzov Rifle Division

Divisional Units

433rd Rifle Regiment
440th Rifle Regiment
451st Rifle Regiment
1029th Artillery Regiment
9th Student Battalion
406th Separate Antitank Artillery Battalion
180th Reconnaissance Company
167th Sapper Battalion
613th Separate Signals Battalion (formally 943rd Sep. Signals Company)
109th Medical Battalion
124th Chemical Defense Company
528th Auto-Transport Company
372nd Field Bakery
843rd Veterinary Field Hospital
1828th Field Postal Station
1151st Field Cash Office of the State Bank

Operations

Stalingrad Strategic Defensive Operation	
Defensive Battles on the near approaches	19.8.1942 - 18.11.1942
Stalingrad Strategic Offensive Operation	
Operation Uranus	19.11.1942 - 30.11.1942
Operation Kol'tso (Ring)	10.1.1943 - 2.2.1943
Smolensk Strategic Offensive Operation	
Smolensk-Roslavl' Army Group Offensive Operation	15.9.1943 - 2.10.1943
Byelorussian Strategic Offensive Operation	
Mogilev Army Group Offensive Operation	23.6.1944 - 28.6.1944
Minsk Army Group Offensive Operation	29.6.1944 - 4.7.1944
Bialystok Army Group Offensive Operation	5.7.1944 - 27.7.1944
Osovetsk Army Group Offensive Operation	6.8.1944 - 14.8.1944
Vistula-Oder Strategic Offensive Operation	
Warsaw-Poznan Army Group Offensive Operation	14.1.1945 - 3.2.1945
Berlin Strategic Offensive Operation	
Seelow-Berlin Army Group Offensive Operation	16.4.1945 - 2.5.1945

Assignments during the Great Patriotic War

Date	Front	Army	Corps
1 March 1942	Moscow Military District	-	-
1 April 1942	Moscow Military District	-	-
1 May 1942	Moscow Military District	-	-
1 June 1942	STAVKA Reserves	8th Reserve Army	-
1 July 1942	STAVKA Reserves	8th Reserve Army	-
1 August 1942	STAVKA Reserves	8th Reserve Army	-
1 September 1942	Stalingrad Front	1st Guards Army	-
1 October 1942	Don Front	66th Army	-
1 November 1942	Don Front	66th Army	-
1 December 1942	Don Front	66th Army	-
1943			
1 January 1943	Don Front	66th Army	-
1 February 1943	STAVKA Reserves	-	-
1 March 1943	Western Front	16th Army	-
1 April 1943	Western Front	16th Army	-
1 May 1943	Western Front	50th Army	-
1 June 1943	Western Front	50th Army	-
1 July 1943	Western Front	50th Army	-
1 August 1943	Western Front	50th Army	-
1 September 1943	Western Front	10th Army	-
1 October 1943	Western Front	10th Army	38th Rifle Corps
1 November 1943	Western Front	10th Army	38th Rifle Corps
1 December 1943	Western Front	10th Army	38th Rifle Corps
1944			
1 January 1944	Western Front	10th Army	38th Rifle Corps
1 February 1944	Western Front	10th Army	38th Rifle Corps
1 March 1944	1st Byelorussian Front	10th Army	38th Rifle Corps
1 April 1944	1st Byelorussian Front	10th Army	38th Rifle Corps
1 May 1944	2nd Byelorussian Front	49th Army	38th Rifle Corps
1 June 1944	2nd Byelorussian Front	49th Army	38th Rifle Corps
1 July 1944	2nd Byelorussian Front	49th Army	70th Rifle Corps
1 August 1944	2nd Byelorussian Front	49th Army	121st Rifle Corps

Date	Front	Army	Corps
1 September 1944	2nd Byelorussian Front	49th Army	-
1 October 1944	STAVKA Reserves	33rd Army	38th Rifle Corps
1 November 1944	1st Byelorussian Fron	33rd Army	38th Rifle Corps
1 December 1944	1st Byelorussian Fron	33rd Army	38th Rifle Corps
1945			
1 January 1945	1st Byelorussian Fron	69th Army	25th Rifle Corps
1 February 1945	1st Byelorussian Fron	33rd Army	38th Rifle Corps
1 March 1945	1st Byelorussian Fron	33rd Army	-
1 April 1945	1st Byelorussian Fron	33rd Army	38th Rifle Corps
1 May 1945	1st Byelorussian Fron	3rd Shock Army	38th Rifle Corps
1 June 1945	Group of Soviet Occupation Forces Germany	3rd Shock Army	38th Rifle Corps

64th Rifle Division (IV)

4th Formation

There is new information that the Division was re-formed in 1955, by the renaming of the 367th Rifle Division. It was assigned to the 6th Army in the Northern Military District. Like all of the Divisions formed in 1955, it did not last long however. The Division, as part of the reorganization of the Soviet Army in 1957, became the 111th Motorized Rifle Division.

Division Commanders

Unknown

Honors and Awards

Division carried over awards from the 367th Rifle Division
None awarded during 1955-1957

Division Honorific Title

64th Red Banner Rifle Division

Divisional Units

Currently unknown, but probably same numbered Regiments as previous Division.

65th Rifle Division (I)

1st Formation

The Division was formed in 1931/32 in Sverdlovsk in the Transbaikal Military District. There is no information so far about the Division before 1939. In August/September of 1939, as part of the partial mobilization conducted by the USSR, it was ordered to form two new Divisions, the 110th and 128th Rifle Divisions, each based around one of the Divisions Rifle Regiments. What remained formed a new 65th Rifle Division.

Active Dates for the Great Patriotic War

None

Division Commanders

Unknown

Honors and Awards

None

Division Honorific Title

64th Rifle Division

Divisional Units

193rd Rifle Regiment
194th Rifle Regiment
195th Rifle Regiment
65th Artillery Regiment

Assignments during the Great Patriotic War

None

65th Rifle Division (II)

2nd Formation

The Division was formed in September 1939 from what remained of the original 65th Rifle Division, which was based around the 193rd Rifle Regiment then stationed in Tyumen. On 22 June 1941 the Division was assigned to the 12th Rifle Corps in the Transbaikal Military District. During July it was assigned to the 36th Army, and in October it was transferred west to the front. On arrival, it was assigned to the 4th Separate Army near Tikhvin (southeast of Leningrad), just in time to participate in the offensive operation there. For its actions during this offensive, the Division won the Order of the Red Banner. By 1 January 1942, the 4th Army was assigned to newly formed Volkhov Front. Later in January it took part in the disastrous Lyuban Offensive Operation which saw the encirclement and destruction of 2nd Shock Army. After a transfer to the 52nd Army, the Division settled in along a quite sector of the front for the rest of 1942 and 1943. On 14 January 1944, the Division participated in the Leningrad-Novgorod Offensive with the 59th Army, which resulted in the liberation of Novgorod, where it won its honorific title. After a refit while in the 3rd Baltic' Front's reserves, the Division was transferred to north to the 7th Army in Karelian Front to participate in the Petsamo-Kirkenes Offensive Operation, which knocked Finland out of the war. For recognition of its actions during this offensive operation the Division was awarded "Guards" status on 29 December 1944 and renamed the 102nd Guards Rifle Division.

Active Dates for the Great Patriotic War

14 November 1941 – 9 November 1944

Division Commanders

11.3.1940 - 22.4.1942	Colonel Petr Kirilovich KOSHEVOI
23.4.1942 - 21.5.1942	Colonel Vasilii Yakovlevich NIKOLAEVSKII
22.5.1942 - 10.8.1942	Colonel Petr Kirilovich KOSHEVOI
11.8.1942 - 30.4.1943	Colonel Vasilii Yakovlevich NIKOLAEVSKII
1.5.1943 - 17.12.1944	Colonel Grigorii Yevstraf'evich
18.12.1944 - 29.12.1944	Colonel Sergei Ivanovich KHRAMTSOV

Honors and Awards

17.12.1941	Awarded the Order of the Red Banner
21.1.1944	Awarded the Honorific designation "Novgorod"

31.10.1944	Awarded the Order of Suvorov II class

Division Honorific Title

65th Novgorod Red Banner Order of Suvorov Rifle Division

Divisional Units

units were awarded their "Guards" designation on 23.1.1945)

	Becomes
38th Rifle Regiment	314th Guards Rifle Regiment
60th Rifle Regiment	316th Guards Rifle Regiment
311th Rifle Regiment	318th Guards Rifle Regiment
127th Artillery Regiment	418th Guards Artillery Regt
172nd Howitzer Artillery Regiment (until 28.1.1942)	
167th Separate Antitank Artillery Battalion	111th Guards Sep. AT Artillery Bn
367th Separate Antiaircraft Artillery Battery (formally 350th Sep. AA Artillery Battalion)	
23rd Reconnaissance Battalion	107th Guards Reconnaissance Co
Separate Ski Battalion (from 13.10.1942 to 10.4.1943)	
74th Sapper Battalion	144th Guards Sapper Battalion
104th Separate Signals Battalion (formally 782nd Sep. Signals Company)	197th Guards Sep. Signals Battalion
54th Medical Battalion	no change
210th Separate Chemical Defense Company	124th Guards Chemical Defense Co
230th Auto-Transport Company	no change
41st Divisional Artillery Workshop Battalion	
163rd Field Bakery (formally 95th Mobile Field Bakery)	no change
199th Veterinary Field Hospital	no change
98th Field Postal Station	no change
281st Field Cash Office of the State Bank	no change

Operations

Tikhvin Strategic Offensive Operation	
Tikhvin-Kirishsk Army Group Offensive Operation	12.11.1941 - 30.12.1941
Lyuban Army Group Offensive Operation	7.1.1942 - 30.4.1942
Rescue of 2nd Shock Army	13.5.1942 - 10.7.1942
Leningrad-Novgorod Strategic Offensive Operation	
Novgorod-Luga Army Group Offensive Operation	14.1.1944 - 15.2.1944
Vyborg-Petrozavodsk Strategic Offensive Operation	
Svir-Petrozavodsk Army Group Offensive Operation	21.6.1944 - 9.8.1944

Assignments during the Great Patriotic War

Date	Front	Army	Corps
22 June 1941	Transbaikal Military District	-	12th Rifle Corps
1 July 1941	Transbaikal Military District	-	12th Rifle Corps
10 July 1941	Transbaikal Military District	-	12th Rifle Corps
1 August 1941	Transbaikal Military District	36th Army	-
1 September 1941	Transbaikal Military District	36th Army	-
1 October 1941	Transbaikal Military District	36th Army	-
1 November 1941	STAVKA Reserves	-	-
1 December 1941	Separate Army	4th Army	-
1942			
1 January 1942	Volkhov Front	4th Army	-
1 February 1942	Volkhov Front	4th Army	-
1 March 1942	Volkhov Front	52nd Army	-
1 April 1942	Volkhov Front	52nd Army	-
1 May 1942	Volkhov Front	52nd Army	-
1 June 1942	Volkhov Front	52nd Army	-
1 July 1942	Volkhov Front	52nd Army	-
1 August 1942	Volkhov Front	52nd Army	-
1 September 1942	Volkhov Front	52nd Army	-
1 October 1942	Volkhov Front	52nd Army	-
1 November 1942	Volkhov Front	52nd Army	-
1 December 1942	Volkhov Front	52nd Army	-
1943			
1 January 1943	Volkhov Front	52nd Army	-
1 February 1943	Volkhov Front	52nd Army	-
1 March 1943	Volkhov Front	52nd Army	-
1 April 1943	Volkhov Front	Front Reserves	-
1 May 1943	Volkhov Front	59th Army	-
1 June 1943	Volkhov Front	59th Army	-
1 July 1943	Volkhov Front	59th Army	-
1 August 1943	Volkhov Front	59th Army	-
1 September 1943	Volkhov Front	59th Army	14th Rifle Corps
1 October 1943	Volkhov Front	59th Army	14th Rifle Corps
1 November 1943	Volkhov Front	59th Army	14th Rifle Corps
1 December 1943	Volkhov Front	59th Army	6th Rifle Corps

Date	Front	Army	Corps
1944			
1 January 1944	Volkhov Front	59th Army	6th Rifle Corps
1 February 1944	Volkhov Front	59th Army	6th Rifle Corps
1 March 1944	Leningrad Front	67th Army	7th Rifle Corps
1 April 1944	Leningrad Front	54th Army	7th Rifle Corps
1 May 1944	3rd Baltic Front	Front Reserves	99th Rifle Corps
1 June 1944	3rd Baltic Front	Front Reserves	99th Rifle Corps
1 July 1944	Karelian Front	7th Army	99th Rifle Corps
1 August 1944	Karelian Front	7th Army	99th Rifle Corps
1 September 1944	Karelian Front	7th Army	99th Rifle Corps
1 October 1944	Karelian Front	7th Army	99th Rifle Corps
1 November 1944	Karelian Front	7th Army	99th Rifle Corps

65th Rifle Division (III)

3rd Formation

There is new information that the Division was re-formed in 1955, by the renaming of the 368th Rifle Division. It was assigned to either the 10th or 42nd Rifle Corps in the Urals Military District. Like all of the Divisions formed in 1955, it did not last long however. The Division, as part of the reorganization of the Soviet Army in 1957, became the 65th Motorized Rifle Division.

Division Commanders

Unknown

Honors and Awards

Division carried over awards from the 368th Rifle Division
None awarded during 1955-1957

Division Honorific Title

65th Lepel Red Banner Rifle Division

Divisional Units

Currently unknown, but probably same numbered Regiments as previous Division.

66th Rifle Division (I)

1st Formation

The Division was formed during July 1936 in the Separate Red Banner Far Eastern Army from cadre of the 2nd Rifle Division. On 22 June 1941 the Division was in the 5th Rifle Corps of the 35th Army in the Far Eastern Front and remained with that army until the start of the Manchurian Strategic Offensive Operation. The 35th Army became part of the 1st Far Eastern Front and the Division fought in the Sungari Army Group Offensive Operation with both 35th Army and 1st Red Banner Army. For its actions during the offensive, the Division was awarded the Order Kutuzov II class. The Division returned to the USSR in October 1945 where it was transferred to the 26th Rifle Corps of the 35th Army. There it began reorganizing into the new 2nd Tank Division, which became the 32nd Tank Division in 1957.

Active Dates for the Great Patriotic War

9 August 1945 - 3 September 1945 as part of the Manchurian Strategic Offensive Operation

Division Commanders

10.1.1939 – 24.1.1942	Colonel Mikhail Kupriyanovich YUSHKEVICH (promoted to General-Major on 9.11.1941)
25.1.1942 – 10.10.1942	Colonel Dmitrii Grigor'evich PISKUNOV
11.10.1942 – 22.11.1944	Colonel Vasilii Flegontovich SOROKOUMOV (promoted to General-Major on 18.5.1943)
23.11.1944 – 3.9.1945	Colonel Fedor Kuz'mich NESTEROV

Honors and Awards

19.9.1945	Awarded the Order of Kutuzov class II

Division Honorific Title

66th Order of Kutuzov Rifle Division

Divisional Units

33rd Rifle Regiment (formerly the 196th Rifle Regiment)
108th Rifle Regiment (formerly the 197th Rifle Regiment)

341st Rifle Regiment (formerly the 198th Rifle Regiment)
161st Artillery Regiment (formerly the 66th Artillery Regiment)
263rd Howitzer Artillery Regiment (until.1.1942)
118th Separate Antitank Artillery Battalion
473rd Separate Antiaircraft Artillery Battalion
39th Reconnaissance Company (formally 39th Reconnaissance Battalion)
91st Sapper Battalion
928th Separate Signals Battalion
42nd Medical Battalion
118th Separate Chemical Defense Company
56th Divisional Artillery Workshop Battalion
44th Mobile Field Hospital
493rd Auto-Transport Company
725th Field Bakery (formally 81st Mobile Field Bakery, 113th Field Bakery)
235th Veterinary Field Hospital (formally 112th Veterinary Field Hospital)
283rd Field Postal Station
255th Field Cash Office of the State Bank

Operations

Manchurian Strategic Offensive Operation
  Sungari Army Group Offensive Operation 9.8.1945 - 2.9.1945

Assignments during the Great Patriotic War

Date	Front	Army	Corps
Jan - Dec 1941	Far Eastern Front	35th Army	-
Jan - Dec 1942	Far Eastern Front	35th Army	-
Jan - Dec 1943	Far Eastern Front	35th Army	5th Rifle Corps
Jan - Dec 1944	Far Eastern Front	35th Army	5th Rifle Corps
Jan - 1 Aug 1945	Far Eastern Front	35th Army	5th Rifle Corps
8 August 1945	1st Far Eastern Front	35th Army	-
3 September 1945	1st Far Eastern Front	1st Red Banner Army	-

66th Rifle Division (II)

2nd Formation

There is new information that the Division was re-formed in 1955, by the renaming of the 371st Rifle Division. It was assigned initially to the 39th Army in the Far East Military District, and then later transferred to the 5th Army. Like all of the Divisions formed in 1955, it did not last long however. The Division, as part of the reorganization of the Soviet Army in 1957, became the 113th Motorized Rifle Division.

Division Commanders

Unknown

Honors and Awards

Division carried over awards from the 371st Rifle Division
None awarded during 1955-1957

Division Honorific Title

66th Vitebsk Red Banner Orders of Suvorov and Kutuzov Rifle Division

Divisional Units

Currently unknown, but probably same numbered Regiments as previous Division.

67th Rifle Division (I)

1st Formation

The Division was formed in 1936 by the renaming of the 20th Territorial Rifle Division, stationed in the Leningrad Military District. It remained there until August/September of 1939 when, as part of the partial mobilization conducted by the USSR, it was ordered to form a new Division, the 155th Rifle Division, based around one of the Divisions Rifle Regiments. What remained formed a new 67th Rifle Division.

Active Dates for the Great Patriotic War

None

Division Commanders

Unknown

Honors and Awards

None

Division Honorific Title

67th Rifle Division

Divisional Units

199th Rifle Regiment
200th Rifle Regiment
201st Rifle Regiment
67th Artillery Regiment

Assignments during the Great Patriotic War

None

67th Rifle Division (II)

2nd Formation

The Division was formed in September 1939 from what remained of the original 67th Rifle Division probably based around the 199th and 200th Rifle Regiments. In October 1939, it was reassigned to the 2nd Special Rifle Corps then located in the Baltic States. The Division took part in the invasion of Latvia in June 1940 and then in August 1940, it was transferred to the new Baltic Special Military District. On 22 June 1941 the Division was in 27th Army in Northwestern Front defending along the coast in Lithuania. It took a beating during the first week of the war and never recovered. The Division was broken up in August and the remaining men used to fill out other divisions within Northwestern Front. It was officially disbanded on 19 September 1941.

Active Dates for the Great Patriotic War

22 June 1941 - 19 September 1941

Division Commanders

14.3.1941 - 21.7.1941	General-Major Nikolai Alekseevich DEDAEV
22.7.1941 - 19.9.1941	Lieutenant Colonel Sergei Fedorovich TOKAREV

Honors and Awards

None

Division Honorific Title

67th Rifle Division

Divisional Units:

56th Rifle Regiment (I)
114th Rifle Regiment
281st Rifle Regiment
94th Artillery Regiment
242nd Howitzer Artillery Regiment
99th Separate Antitank Artillery Battalion
389th Separate Antiaircraft Artillery Battalion

11th Reconnaissance Battalion
83rd Sapper Battalion
36th Separate Signals Battalion
72nd Medical Battalion
275th Separate Chemical Defense Company
64th Auto-Transport Battalion
56th Mobile Field Bakery
583rd Field Cash Office of the State Bank

Operations

Baltic Strategic Defensive Operation	
Border Defensive Battles	22.6.1941 – 24.6.1941
Shyaulyai Army Group Offensive Operation	24.6.1941 – 27.6.1941
Leningrad Strategic Defensive Operation	
Kingisepp-Luga Army Group Defensive Operation	10.7.1941 – 10.8.1941

Assignments during the Great Patriotic War

Date	Front	Army	Corps
22 June 1941	Northwestern Front	27th Army	-
1 July 1941	Northwestern Front	27th Army	-
10 July 1941	Northwestern Front	8th Army	-

67th Rifle Division (III)

3rd Formation

The Division was formed on 20 September 1941 in the 7th Separate Army defending against the Finns in the Karelian region along the Svir River line. It remained there in relative quite until February 1944, and then was transferred to 19th Army in the Karelian Front. In October, the Division was assigned to the 14th Separate Army and became a garrison unit in the Artic circle region in Finland and Norway. After the war it remained in the Belomorsk, later Northern Military District until 1957 when it was reorganized into the 116th Motorized Rifle Division.

Active Dates for the Great Patriotic War

20 September 1941 - 9 May 1945

Division Commanders

20.9.1941 - 17.10.1941	Unknown
18.10.1941 - 20.9.1944	Lieutenant Colonel Sergei Fedorovich TOKAREV (promoted to Colonel on 4.12.1941) (promoted to General-Major on 1.9.1943)
21.9.1944 - 21.6.1945	Colonel Yakov Yakovlevich ZAPIRICH

Honors and Awards

None

Division Honorific Title

67th Rifle Division

Divisional Units

9th Rifle Regiment (until 19.12.1943)
56th Rifle Regiment (II) (from 20.12.1943)
452nd Rifle Regiment
719th Rifle Regiment
3rd Artillery Regiment
99th Separate Antitank Artillery Battalion
759th Mortar Battalion (from 1.2.1942 to 8.11.1942)

11th Reconnaissance Company
83rd Sapper Battalion
36th Separate Signals Battalion (formally 297th Sep. Signals Company)
72nd Medical Battalion
275th Separate Chemical Defense Company
178th Auto-Transport Company
154th Field Bakery
31st Veterinary Field Hospital
194th Field Postal Station
583rd Field Cash Office of the State Bank

Operations

No major operations

Assignments during the Great Patriotic War

Date	Front	Army	Corps
1 October 1941	Separate Army	7th Army	-
1 November 1941	Separate Army	7th Army	-
1 December 1941	Separate Army	7th Army	-
1942			
1 January 1942	Separate Army	7th Army	-
1 February 1942	Separate Army	7th Army	-
1 March 1942	Separate Army	7th Army	-
1 April 1942	Separate Army	7th Army	-
1 May 1942	Separate Army	7th Army	-
1 June 1942	Separate Army	7th Army	-
1 July 1942	Separate Army	7th Army	-
1 August 1942	Separate Army	7th Army	-
1 September 1942	Separate Army	7th Army	-
1 October 1942	Separate Army	7th Army	4th Rifle Corps
1 November 1942	Separate Army	7th Army	4th Rifle Corps
1 December 1942	Separate Army	7th Army	4th Rifle Corps
1943			
1 January 1943	Separate Army	7th Army	-
1 February 1943	Separate Army	7th Army	-
1 March 1943	Separate Army	7th Army	-
1 April 1943	Separate Army	7th Army	-
1 May 1943	Separate Army	7th Army	-
1 June 1943	Separate Army	7th Army	-
1 July 1943	Separate Army	7th Army	-
1 August 1943	Separate Army	7th Army	-
1 September 1943	Separate Army	7th Army	-
1 October 1943	Separate Army	7th Army	-

Date	Front	Army	Corps
1 November 1943	Separate Army	7th Army	-
1 December 1943	Separate Army	7th Army	-
1944			
1 January 1944	Separate Army	7th Army	-
1 February 1944	Separate Army	7th Army	4th Rifle Corps
1 March 1944	Karelian Front	19th Army	-
1 April 1944	Karelian Front	19th Army	-
1 May 1944	Karelian Front	19th Army	-
1 June 1944	Karelian Front	19th Army	-
1 July 1944	Karelian Front	19th Army	-
1 August 1944	Karelian Front	19th Army	-
1 September 1944	Karelian Front	19th Army	-
1 October 1944	Karelian Front	19th Army	133rd Rifle Corps
1 November 1944	Karelian Front	14th Army	133rd Rifle Corps
1 December 1944	Separate Army	14th Army	131st Rifle Corps
1945			
1 January 1945	Separate Army	14th Army	131st Rifle Corps
1 February 1945	Separate Army	14th Army	131st Rifle Corps
1 March 1945	Separate Army	14th Army	131st Rifle Corps
1 April 1945	Separate Army	14th Army	131st Rifle Corps
1 May 1945	Separate Army	14th Army	131st Rifle Corps

68th Rifle Division

There is new information that the Division was formed in 1955 (previously, the Number 68 was used for a Mountain Rifle Division), by the renaming of the 372nd Rifle Division. It was assigned to the 11th Guards Rifle Corps in the Voronezh Military District. Like all of the Divisions formed in 1955, it did not last long however. The Division, as part of the reorganization of the Soviet Army in 1957, became the 117th Motorized Rifle Division.

Division Commanders

Unknown

Honors and Awards

Division carried over awards from the 372nd Rifle Division
None awarded during 1955-1957

Division Honorific Title:

68th Red Banner Rifle Division

Divisional Units

Currently unknown, but probably same numbered Regiments as previous Division.

69th Rifle Division (I)

1st Formation

The Division was form in the early 1936 in the Kharbarovsk region of the Far East from a cadre provided by the 3rd Rifle Division. In March 1941 the Division was reformed as a Motorized Rifle Division.

Active Dates for the Great Patriotic War

None

Division Commanders

Unknown

Honors and Awards

None

Division Honorific Title

69th Rifle Division

Divisional Units

205th Rifle Regiment
206th Rifle Regiment
207th Rifle Regiment
69th Artillery Regiment

Assignments during the Great Patriotic War

None

69th Rifle Division (II)

2nd Formation

The Division was formed on 14 February 1942 by renaming the 461st Rifle Division in the Central Asian Military District. By mid-February, the Division started moving west and was placed in STAVKA Reserves. Upon its arrival near the front, it was assigned to the 50th Army in Western Front. It remained with the 50th Army along a quite sector of the front until February 1943 when it was transferred to 65th Army in the Central Front. The Division was defending the Western side of the Kursk salient during the Battle of Kursk. In October 1943, it participated in the Byelorussian Strategic Offensive Operation, pushing the Germans back to the Dnepr in the area just south of Gomel. By this time (20.10.43) the Central Front had been renamed the Byelorussian Front. The Division also won its honorific for the liberation of Sevsk. In January 1944, it participated in the Kalinkovichi-Mozyr Army Group Operation, establishing a bridgehead over the Dnepr for future offensives, and was awarded the Order of Suvorov II class. In June 1944, the Division participated in the Byelorussian Strategic Offensive Operation and the Lublin-Brest Offensive, advancing to the outskirts of Warsaw. For its actions during these battles, the Division was awarded the Order of the Red Banner. In November of 1944, the 65th Army was transferred to 2nd Byelorussian Front and remained there until the end of the war. In January 1945, it participated in the East Prussian Offensive and then the East Pomeranian Offensive, helping to capture Danzig. Finally it participated in the Berlin Strategic Offensive, ending the war on the Baltic coast near Rubnitz. On 29 May by STAVKA Order No. 11097 the Division became part of the Northern Group of Forces and station near Lodz. It returned to the USSR in 1947 and was transferred to the Northern Military where it was initially assigned to the 44th Rifle Corps. In 1957, it was reorganized into the 69th Motorized Rifle Division.

Active Dates for the Great Patriotic War

1 April 1942 – 4 February 1943
18 February 1943 – 9 May 1945

Division Commanders

14.2.1942 – 4.1.1943	Brigade Commander Mikhail Andreevich BOGDANOV (promoted to General-Major on 1.10.1942)
5.1.1943 – 5.12.1943	Colonel Ivan Aleksandrovich KUZOVKOV (promoted to General-Major on 1.9.1943)
6.12.1943 – 6.9.1944	General-Major Iosif Iustinovich SANKOVSKII

7.9.1944 - 9.5.1945 Colonel Fedor Alekseevich MAKAROV (promoted to General-Major on 2.11.1944)

Honors and Awards

19.6.1943	Awarded the Order of the Red Banner
31.8.1943	Awarded the Honorific designation "Sevsk"
15.1.1944	Awarded the Order of Suvorov II class
25.7.1944	Awarded the Order of the Red Banner
4.6.1945	Awarded the Order of Kutuzov II class

Division Honorific Title

69th Sevsk twice Red Banner Orders of Suvorov and Kutuzov Rifle Division

Divisional Units

120th Rifle Regiment
237th Rifle Regiment
303rd Rifle Regiment
118th Artillery Regiment
109th Separate Antitank Artillery Battalion
161st Mortar Battalion (until 18.10.1942)
20th Reconnaissance Company
99th Sapper Battalion
41st Separate Signals Battalion (formally 15th Sep. Signals Company)
71st Medical Battalion
102nd Auto-Transport Company
925th Veterinary Field Hospital
802nd Field Postal Station (formally 1706th Field Postal Station)
1102nd Field Cash Office of the State Bank

Operations

Chernigov-Poltava Strategic Offensive Operation	
Chernigov-Pripyet Army Group Offensive Operation	26.8.1943 - 30.9.1943
Byelorussian Strategic Offensive Operation	
Gomel'sko-Rechitskaia Army Group Offensive Operation	30.9.1943 - 30.10.1943
Gomel'sko-Rechitskaia Army Group Offensive Operation	10.11.1943 - 30.11.1943
Kalinkovichi Army Group Offensive Operation	8.12.1943 - 11.12.1943
Kalinkovichi Army Group Offensive Operation	20.12.1943 - 27.12.1943
Kalinkovichi-Mozyr Army Group Offensive Operation	8.1.1944 - 30.1.1944
Byelorussian Strategic Offensive Operation	
Bobruisk Army Group Offensive Operation	23.6.1944- 29.6.1944
Lublin-Brest Army Group Offensive Operation	18.7.1944 - 2.8.1944
East Prussian Strategic Offensive Operation	
Mlawo-Elbing Army Group Offensive Operation	14.1.1945 - 26.1.1945

East Pomeranian Strategic Offensive Operation
Chojnice-Koeslin Army Group Offensive Operation 10.2.1945 – 6.3.1945
Danzig Army Group Offensive Operation 7.3.1945 – 31.3.1945
Berlin Strategic Offensive Operation
Settin-Rostock Army Group Offensive Operation 16.4.1945 – 8.5.1945

Assignments during the Great Patriotic War

Date	Front	Army	Corps
1 January 1942	Central Asian Military District	-	-
1 February 1942	Central Asian Military District	-	-
1 March 1942	STAVKA Reserves	-	-
1 April 1942	Western Front	Front Reserves	-
1 May 1942	Western Front	50th Army	-
1 June 1942	Western Front	50th Army	-
1 July 1942	Western Front	50th Army	-
1 August 1942	Western Front	50th Army	-
1 September 1942	Western Front	50th Army	-
1 October 1942	Western Front	50th Army	-
1 November 1942	Western Front	50th Army	-
1 December 1942	Western Front	50th Army	-
1943			
1 January 1943	Western Front	50th Army	-
1 February 1943	Western Front	50th Army	-
1 March 1943	Central Front	65th Army	-
1 April 1943	Central Front	65th Army	-
1 May 1943	Central Front	65th Army	-
1 June 1943	Central Front	65th Army	-
1 July 1943	Central Front	65th Army	18th Rifle Corps
1 August 1943	Central Front	65th Army	18th Rifle Corps
1 September 1943	Central Front	65th Army	19th Rifle Corps
1 October 1943	Central Front	65th Army	18th Rifle Corps
1 November 1943	Byelorussian Front	65th Army	18th Rifle Corps
1 December 1943	Byelorussian Front	65th Army	18th Rifle Corps
1944			
1 January 1944	Byelorussian Front	65th Army	18th Rifle Corps
1 February 1944	Byelorussian Front	65th Army	18th Rifle Corps
1 March 1944	1st Byelorussian Front	65th Army	18th Rifle Corps
1 April 1944	1st Byelorussian Front	65th Army	18th Rifle Corps
1 May 1944	1st Byelorussian Front	65th Army	18th Rifle Corps
1 June 1944	1st Byelorussian Front	65th Army	18th Rifle Corps

Date	Front	Army	Corps
1 July 1944	1st Byelorussian Front	65th Army	18th Rifle Corps
1 August 1944	1st Byelorussian Front	65th Army	18th Rifle Corps
1 September 1944	1st Byelorussian Front	65th Army	18th Rifle Corps
1 October 1944	1st Byelorussian Front	65th Army	18th Rifle Corps
1 November 1944	1st Byelorussian Front	65th Army	18th Rifle Corps
1 December 1944	2nd Byelorussian Front	65th Army	18th Rifle Corps
1945			
1 January 1945	2nd Byelorussian Front	65th Army	18th Rifle Corps
1 February 1945	2nd Byelorussian Front	65th Army	18th Rifle Corps
1 March 1945	2nd Byelorussian Front	65th Army	18th Rifle Corps
1 April 1945	2nd Byelorussian Front	65th Army	18th Rifle Corps
1 May 1945	2nd Byelorussian Front	65th Army	18th Rifle Corps
1 June 1945	Northern Group of Forces	65th Army	18th Rifle Corps

70th Rifle Division (I)

1st Formation

The Division was formed in Kuibyshev in 1934 based on cadre of the 34th Rifle Division. In August/September of 1939, as part of the partial mobilization conducted by the USSR, it was ordered to form a new Division, the 117th Rifle Division, based around one of the Divisions Rifle Regiments. What remained formed a new 70th Rifle Division.

Active Dates for the Great Patriotic War

None

Division Commanders

Unknown

Honors and Awards

None

Division Honorific Title

70th Rifle Division

Divisional Units

208th Rifle Regiment
209th Rifle Regiment
210th Rifle Regiment
70th Artillery Regiment

Assignments during the Great Patriotic War

None

70th Rifle Division (II)

2nd Formation

The Division was formed in September 1939 from what remained of the original 70th Rifle Division probably based around the 208th Rifle Regiment. During the Winter War with Finland, the Division was part of 7th Army, 19th Rifle Corps. For its actions in breaking the Mannerheim Line, it was awarded the Order of Lenin on 21 March 1940. On 22 June 1941 the Division was in the Northern Front, 23rd Army, 50th Rifle Corps, and in reserve near Leningrad. In July it was defending against the German push to cross the Luga River. By September the Division was assigned to 55th Army and was defending along the Neva River near Leningrad. In April 1942, it was part of the Neva Operations Group and in early October 1942, the Division participated in a failed offensive to break the siege. For recognition of its actions during the offensive, the Division was awarded "Guards" status on 16 October 1942 and renamed 45th Guards Rifle Division.

Active Dates for the Great Patriotic War

22 June 1941 - 16 October 1942

Division Commanders

1.7.1940 - 15.7.1941	General-Major Andrei Yegorovich FEDYUNIN
16.7.1941 - 21.12.1941	Major Vyacheslav Petrovich YAKUTOVICH (promoted to Colonel on 8.11.1941)
22.12.1941 - 8.1.1942	Unknown
9.1.1942 - 7.4.1942	Colonel Yevgenii Yefimovich TSUKANOV
8.4.1942 - 16.10.1942	Colonel Anatolii Andreevich KRASNOV

Honors and Awards

21.3.1940	Awarded the Order of Lenin
October 1940	Awarded the Order of the Red Banner

Division Honorific Title

70th Red Banner Order of Lenin Rifle Division

Divisional Units

units were awarded their "Guards" designation on 28.10.1942)

	Becomes
68th Rifle Regiment (I)	129th Guards Rifle Regiment
252nd Rifle Regiment (I)	131st Guards Rifle Regiment
329th Rifle Regiment (I)	134th Guards Rifle Regiment
221st Artillery Regiment (until 20.12.1941)	
227th Howitzer Artillery Regiment (transformed into an Artillery Regiment)	96th Guards Artillery Regiment
94th Separate Antitank Artillery Battalion	50th Guards Sep. AT Artillery Bn
340th Separate Antiaircraft Artillery Battery (formally 198th Sep. AA Artillery Battalion)	
65th Reconnaissance Battalion	43rd Guards Reconnaissance Co
64th Sapper Battalion	49th Guards Sapper Battalion
11th Separate Signals Battalion	71st Guards Sep. Signals Battalion
21st Medical Battalion	521st Medical Battalion
36th Separate Chemical Defense Company	47th Guards Chemical Defense Co
34th Auto-Transport Company	605th Auto-Transport Company
32nd Field Bakery (formally 165th Field Bakery)	635th Field Bakery
77th Veterinary Field Hospital	638th Veterinary Field Hospital
121st Field Postal Station	no change
192nd Field Cash Office of the State Bank	no change

Operations

Leningrad Strategic Defensive Operation	
Sol'tsy-Dno Army Group Offensive Operation	15.7.1941 – 20.7.1941
Staraia-Russa Army Group Offensive Operation	8.8.1941 – 23.8.1941
Sinyavino Army Group Offensive Operation	19.8.1942 – 10.10.1942

Assignments during the Great Patriotic War

Date	Front	Army	Corps
22 June 1941	Northern Front	23rd Army	50th Rifle Corps
1 July 1941	Northern Front	Front Reserves	-
10 July 1941	Northwestern Front	11th Army	16th Rifle Corps
1 August 1941	Northwestern Front	Novgorod Operations Group	16th Rifle Corps
1 September 1941	Leningrad Front	55th Army	-
1 October 1941	Leningrad Front	55th Army	-
1 November 1941	Leningrad Front	55th Army	-
1 December 1941	Leningrad Front	55th Army	-
1942			
1 January 1942	Leningrad Front	55th Army	-

Date	Front	Army	Corps
1 February 1942	Leningrad Front	55th Army	-
1 March 1942	Leningrad Front	55th Army	-
1 April 1942	Leningrad Front	55th Army	-
1 May 1942	Leningrad Front	Neva Operations Group	-
1 June 1942	Leningrad Front	Neva Operations Group	-
1 July 1942	Leningrad Front	Neva Operations Group	-
1 August 1942	Leningrad Front	Neva Operations Group	-
1 September 1942	Leningrad Front	Neva Operations Group	-
1 October 1942	Leningrad Front	Neva Operations Group	-

70th Rifle Division (III)

3rd Formation

The Division was formed on 14 April 1943 from cadre of the 47th and 146th Separate Rifle Brigades in the Moscow Military District near Kaluga. The Division was assigned to 3rd Reserve Army in STAVKA Reserves for training. Sent to the Western Front in July 1943, it participated in the Smolensk Offensive Operation advancing with the 33rd Army toward the Dnepr River near Gorki. In September the Division was transfer to 49th Army in Western Front and remained there until Western Front became the 2nd Byelorussian Front in April 1944. At this time it was transferred back to 33rd Army and participated in the Byelorussian Offensive winning its honorific title and advancing into Lithuania. Transferred to 1st Baltic Front in August of 1944 it was assigned to 43rd Army in October. The Division took part in the Baltic Offensive Operation pushing Army Group North back to the Kurland Peninsula. In January 1945 it participated in the East Prussian Offensive advancing toward Königsberg. The Division ended the war in 2nd Byelorussian Front with 43rd Army. It became part of the Northern Group of Forces in June 1945. Although it cannot be confirmed at this time, it is believed it was disbanded when the 43rd Army withdrew from Poland in 1946.

Active Dates for the Great Patriotic War

12 July 1943 - 23 July 1943
1 August 1943 - 9 May 1945

Division Commanders

14.4.1943 - 9.2.1944	Colonel Makhmud Abdul-Rza ABILOV
10.2.1944 - 12.3.1944	Colonel Kornilii Fedorovich RAKHMANOV
13.3.1944 - 14.3.1944	Unknown
15.3.1944 - 27.5.1944	Colonel Makhmud Abdul-Rza ABILOV
28.5.1944 - 17.7.1944	Colonel Mikhail Mefod'evich KOLESNIKOV
18.7.1944 - 21.7.1944	Unknown
22.7.1944 - 9.5.1945	Colonel Serafim Andrianovich KRASNOVSKII

Honors and Awards

10.7.1944	Awarded the Honorific designation "Verzhnedneprovskaia"
22.10.1944	Awarded the Order of Suvorov II class

Division Honorific Title

70th Verzhnedneprovskaia Order of Suvorov Rifle Division

Divisional Units

68th Rifle Regiment (II)
252nd Rifle Regiment (II)
329th Rifle Regiment (II)
227th Artillery Regiment
91st Separate Antitank Artillery Battalion
65th Reconnaissance Company
64th Sapper Battalion
553rd Separate Signals Battalion (formally 650th Sep. Signals Company)
21st Medical Battalion
36th Separate Chemical Defense Company
176th Auto-Transport Company
165th Field Bakery
286th Veterinary Field Hospital
1605th Field Postal Station
1663rd Field Cash Office of the State Bank

Operations

Smolensk Strategic Offensive Operation	
Spas-Demensk Army Group Offensive Operation	7.8.1943 - 20.8.1943
Yelnia-Dorogobuzh Army Group Offensive Operation	28.8.1943 - 6.9.1943
Smolensk-Roslavl' Army Group Offensive Operation	15.9.1943 - 2.10.1943
Byelorussian Strategic Offensive Operation	
Mogilev Army Group Offensive Operation	23.6.1944 - 28.6.1944
Minsk Army Group Offensive Operation	29.6.1944 - 4.7.1944
Bialystok Army Group Offensive Operation	5.7.1944 - 27.7.1944
Baltic Strategic Offensive Operation	
Riga Army Group Offensive Operation	14.9.1944 - 24.10.1944
Memel Army Group Offensive Operation	27.9.1944 - 24.11.1944
East Prussian Strategic Offensive Operation	
Königsberg Army Group Offensive Operation	6.4.1945 - 9.4.1945

Assignments during the Great Patriotic War

Date	Front	Army	Corps
1 May 1943	STAVKA Reserves	3rd Reserve Army	-
1 June 1943	STAVKA Reserves	3rd Reserve Army	-
1 July 1943	STAVKA Reserves	3rd Reserve Army	-
1 August 1943	Western Front	21st Army	-
1 September 1943	Western Front	33rd Army	70th Rifle Corps
1 October 1943	Western Front	49th Army	62nd Rifle Corps

Date	Front	Army	Corps
1 November 1943	Western Front	49th Army	62nd Rifle Corps
1 December 1943	Western Front	49th Army	113th Rifle Corps
1944			
1 January 1944	Western Front	49th Army	113th Rifle Corps
1 February 1944	Western Front	49th Army	113th Rifle Corps
1 March 1944	Western Front	49th Army	113th Rifle Corps
1 April 1944	Western Front	49th Army	113th Rifle Corps
1 May 1944	2nd Byelorussian Front	33rd Army	62nd Rifle Corps
1 June 1944	2nd Byelorussian Front	33rd Army	62nd Rifle Corps
1 July 1944	2nd Byelorussian Front	33rd Army	62nd Rifle Corps
1 August 1944	3rd Byelorussian Front	33rd Army	62nd Rifle Corps
1 September 1944	1st Baltic Front	Front Reserve	19th Rifle Corps
1 October 1944	1st Baltic Front	43rd Army	19th Rifle Corps
1 November 1944	1st Baltic Front	43rd Army	19th Rifle Corps
1 December 1944	1st Baltic Front	43rd Army	19th Rifle Corps
1945			
1 January 1945	1st Baltic Front	43rd Army	19th Rifle Corps
1 February 1945	1st Baltic Front	4th Shock Army	19th Rifle Corps
1 March 1945	3rd Byelorussian Front	Front Reserves	-
1 April 1945	3rd Byelorussian Front – Zemland Group of Forces	43rd Army	90th Rifle Corps
1 May 1945	2nd Byelorussian Front	43rd Army	90th Rifle Corps
1 June 1945	Northern Group of Forces	43rd Army	90th Rifle Corps

70th Rifle Division (IV)

4th Formation

The Division was formed in 1955 in the Turkestan Military District by the renumbering of the 374th Rifle Division. It remained in the District for its entire life, which ended in 1957 when it was part of the complete reorganization of the Soviet ground forces. At that time, it was reorganized to the 140th Motorized Rifle Division, which would be disbanded in 1959.

Active Dates for the Great Patriotic War

None

Division Commanders

Unknown

Honors and Awards

Division carried over awards from the 374th Rifle Division

Unknown	Order of Red Banner

Division Honorific Title

70th Lyubanskaya Red Banner Rifle Division

Divisional Units

Unknown

Assignments during the Great Patriotic War

None

71st Rifle Division (I)

1st Formation

The Division was formed in 1934 in the Siberian Military District. On 9 January 1935, it received the honorific "in the name of the Kuzbass Proleteriat". In August/September of 1939, as part of the partial mobilization conducted by the USSR, it was ordered to form two new Divisions, the 107th and 194th Rifle Divisions, based around two of the Divisions Rifle Regiments. What remained formed a new 71st Rifle Division.

Active Dates for the Great Patriotic War

None

Division Commanders

Unknown

Honors and Awards

9.1.1935	Awarded the Honorific designation "in the name of the Kuzbass Proletariat"

Division Honorific Title

70th Rifle Division in the name of the Kuzbass Proletariat

Divisional Units

211th Rifle Regiment
212th Rifle Regiment
213th Rifle Regiment
71st Artillery Regiment

Assignments during the Great Patriotic War

None

71st Rifle Division (II)

2nd Formation

The Division was formed in September 1939 from what remained of the original 71st Rifle Division probably based around the 211th Rifle Regiment. The Division was disbanded in January 1940.

Active Dates for the Great Patriotic War

None

Division Commanders

Unknown

Honors and Awards

None

Division Honorific Title

71st Rifle Division

Divisional Units

Unknown

Assignments during the Great Patriotic War

None

71st Rifle Division (III)

3rd Formation

The Division was formed on 10 June 1940 by renaming the Special Karelo-Finnish Rifle Division. It remained there through the pre-war period. On 22 June 1941 the Division was stationed along the border with Finland on the Karelian Isthmus and was assigned to 7th Army in Northern Front. It retreated to north of Lake Onega and by October it was assigned to the Medvezhegorskaya Operations Group, Karelian Front. In March, the Group was renamed 32nd Army and the Division remained with it along a quite sector until it was sent south in October. At this time, the Division was transferred to Volkhov Front and placed in the front reserves until December when it was assigned to the 2nd Shock Army. In April, the Division was again moved south, assigned to the 27th Army, and placed in the Steppe Military District. It was sent to the front as part of Voronezh Front in late July and participated in both the Belgorod-Khar'kov and Kiev Offensives. On 20 October 1943, the Voronezh Front was renamed the 1st Ukrainian Front. In December 1943, the Division was transferred to 18th Army and participated in the Zhitmir-Berdichev and the Proskurov-Chernovtsy Army Group Offensive Operations. In March, it was transferred to the 13th Army, and after a rest and refit, it took part in the L'vov-Sandomierz Offensive, establishing a bridgehead over the Vistula River. For its actions in this operation, it was awarded the Order of the Red Banner. After a short stay in STAVKA Reserves to again refit, the Division was again sent to the front with the 65th Army and then assigned to the 70th Army in the 2nd Byelorussian Front. The Division now participated in both the East Prussian and East Pomeranian Offensives and then the Berlin Offensive, ending the war on the line of contact with the British near Schwerin, Germany. The 70th Army was then transferred to 1st Byelorussian Front and then became part of the Group of Soviet Occupation Forces in Germany by STAVKA Order No. 11095. In the same order, it was ordered to disbanded, but for some reason this was rescinded. By November 1945, the Division, along with most of the 70th Army, had been transferred to the South-Urals Military District. Shortly thereafter, it was transferred to Petrozavodsk in the Northern Military District where it was assigned to the 6th Combined-Arms Army. It remained there until 1957 when it was reorganized to the 71st Motorized Rifle Division.

Active Dates for the Great Patriotic War

22 June 1941 – 30 April 1943
9 July 1943 – 7 September 1944
1 October 1944 - 9 May 1945

Division Commanders

2.1.1941 - 23.8.1941	Colonel Vasilii Nikolaevich FEDOROV
25.8.1941 - 2.1.1942	Colonel Mikhail Fedoseevich PEPELYAEV
3.1.1942 - 5.1.1943	Colonel Vasilii Nikolaevich FEDOROV
6.1.1943 - 21.11.1943	General-Major Nikifor Matveevich ZAMIROVSKII
22.11.1943 - 4.7.1944	Colonel Nikolai Zakharovich BELYAEV
5.7.1944 - 28.7.1944	Colonel Vasilii Fedorovich TRUNIN
29.7.1944 - 5.8.1944	Unknown
6.8.1944 - 9.5.1945	Colonel Nikolai Zakharovich BELYAEV

Honors and Awards

5.4.1945	Awarded the Honorific designation "Torun'skaia"
22.10.1944	Awarded the Order of Red Banner

Division Honorific Title

71st Torun'skaia Red Banner Rifle Division

Divisional Units

52nd Rifle Regiment (until 27.9.1941, transferred to 37th Rifle Division)
126th Rifle Regiment
367th Rifle Regiment
131st Rifle Regiment from 27.7.1941, transferred to 78th Rifle Division 10.10.1941)
20th Rifle Regiment (transferred from 37th Rifle Division, 3.1.1942 until 1.3.1942, transferred back to 37th Rifle Division)
230th Light Artillery Regiment (until.10.1941)
237th Artillery Regiment (from the 237th Howitzer Artillery Regiment.12.1941)
237th Howitzer Artillery Regiment (until.12.1941, reorganized as an Artillery Regiment)
133rd Separate Antitank Artillery Battalion
271st Separate Antiaircraft Artillery Battalion
367th Mortar Battalion (from 29.11.1941 to 19.10.1942)
74th Reconnaissance Company (formally 74th Reconnaissance Battalion)
128th Sapper Battalion
126th Separate Signals Battalion (formally 628th Sep. Signals Company)
69th Medical Battalion
17th Separate Chemical Defense Company
193rd Auto-Transport Company (formally 19th Auto-Transport Battalion)
166th Field Bakery (formally 29th Mobile Field Bakery)
256th Veterinary Field Hospital
193rd Field Artillery Repair Shop
234th Field Postal Station
193rd Field Cash Office of the State Bank

Operations

Artic-Karelia Strategic Defensive Operation	
Defensive Battles near Petrozavodsk	1.7.1941 – 10.10.1941
Operation Iskra (Spark)	12.1.1943 – 30.1.1943
Belgorod-Khar'kov Strategic Offensive Operation	
Belgorod-Bogodukhov Army Group Offensive Operation	3.8.1943 – 23.8.1943
Chernigov-Poltava Strategic Offensive Operation	
Sumy-Priluki Army Group Offensive Operation	26.8.1943 – 30.9.1943
Kiev Strategic Offensive Operation	
Lyutezh Army Group Offensive Operation	11.10.1943 – 24.10.1943
Kiev Strategic Offensive Operation	3.11.1943 – 13.11.1943
Kiev Strategic Defensive Operation	13.11.1943 – 22.12.1943
Dnepr-Carpathian Strategic Offensive Operation	
Zhitomir-Berdichev Army Group Offensive Operation	24.12.1943 – 14.1.1944
Proskurov-Chernovtsy Army Group Offensive Operation	4.3.1944 - 17.4.1944
L'vov-Sandomierz Strategic Offensive Operation	
L'vov Army Group Offensive Operation	13.7.1944 – 27.7.1944
Sandomierz Army Group Offensive Operation	28.7.1944 – 29.8.1944
East Prussian Strategic Offensive Operation	
Mlawo-Elbing Army Group Offensive Operation	14.1.1945 – 26.1.1945
East Pomeranian Strategic Offensive Operation	
Chojnice-Koeslin Army Group Offensive Operation	10.2.1945 – 6.3.1945
Danzig Army Group Offensive Operation	7.3.1945 – 31.3.1945
Berlin Strategic Offensive Operation	
Settin-Rostock Army Group Offensive Operation	16.4.1945 – 8.5.1945

Assignments during the Great Patriotic War

Date	Front	Army	Corps
22 June 1941	Northern Front	7th Army	-
1 July 1941	Northern Front	7th Army	-
10 July 1941	Northern Front	7th Army	-
1 August 1941	Northern Front	7th Army	-
1 September 1941	Northern Front	7th Army	-
1 October 1941	Separate Army	7th Army	-
1 November 1941	Karelian Front	Medvezhegorskaya Operations Group	-
1 December 1941	Karelian Front	Medvezhegorskaya Operations Group	-
1942			
1 January 1942	Karelian Front	Medvezhegorskaya Operations Group	-
1 February 1942	Karelian Front	Medvezhegorskaya Operations Group	-

Date	Front	Army	Corps
1 March 1942	Karelian Front	Medvezhegorskaya Operations Group	-
1 April 1942	Karelian Front	32nd Army	-
1 May 1942	Karelian Front	32nd Army	-
1 June 1942	Karelian Front	32nd Army	-
1 July 1942	Karelian Front	32nd Army	-
1 August 1942	Karelian Front	32nd Army	-
1 September 1942	Karelian Front	32nd Army	-
1 October 1942	Karelian Front	32nd Army	-
1 November 1942	Volkhov Front	Front Reserves	-
1 December 1942	Volkhov Front	Front Reserves	-
1943			
1 January 1943	Volkhov Front	2nd Shock Army	-
1 February 1943	Volkhov Front	2nd Shock Army	-
1 March 1943	Volkhov Front	2nd Shock Army	-
1 April 1943	Volkhov Front	2nd Shock Army	-
1 May 1943	STAVKA Reserves	27th Army	-
1 June 1943	Steppe Military District	27th Army	-
1 July 1943	Steppe Military District	27th Army	-
1 August 1943	Voronezh Front	27th Army	-
1 September 1943	Voronezh Front	27th Army	-
1 October 1943	Voronezh Front	38th Army	50th Rifle Corps
1 November 1943	1st Ukrainian Front	38th Army	21st Rifle Corps
1 December 1943	1st Ukrainian Front	38th Army	21st Rifle Corps
1944			
1 January 1944	1st Ukrainian Front	18th Army	22nd Rifle Corps
1 February 1944	1st Ukrainian Front	18th Army	22nd Rifle Corps
1 March 1944	1st Ukrainian Front	18th Army	22nd Rifle Corps
1 April 1944	1st Ukrainian Front	13th Army	24th Rifle Corps
1 May 1944	1st Ukrainian Front	13th Army	24th Rifle Corps
1 June 1944	1st Ukrainian Front	13th Army	24th Rifle Corps
1 July 1944	1st Ukrainian Front	13th Army	24th Rifle Corps
1 August 1944	1st Ukrainian Front	13th Army	24th Rifle Corps
1 September 1944	1st Ukrainian Front	13th Army	24th Rifle Corps
1 October 1944	STAVKA Reserves	6th Army	47th Rifle Corps
1 November 1944	1st Byelorussian Front	65th Army	47th Rifle Corps
1 December 1944	2nd Byelorussian Front	65th Army	47th Rifle Corps
1945			
1 January 1945	2nd Byelorussian Front	70th Army	47th Rifle Corps
1 February 1945	2nd Byelorussian Front	70th Army	47th Rifle Corps
1 March 1945	2nd Byelorussian Front	70th Army	47th Rifle Corps

Date	Front	Army	Corps
1 April 1945	2nd Byelorussian Front	70th Army	47th Rifle Corps
1 May 1945	2nd Byelorussian Front	70th Army	47th Rifle Corps
1 June 1945	Group of Northern Forces	70th Army	47th Rifle Corps
1 July 1945	Group of Soviet Occupation Forces Germany	70th Army	47th Rifle Corps

72nd Rifle Division (I)

1st Formation

The Division was formed in 1936/37 in Vinnitsa in the Kiev Military District. In September 1939 it participated in the invasion of Poland as part of 13th Rifle Corps in 12th Army. And then in December of 1939, the Division was transferred to the Front during the Soviet-Finnish War. In June 1940, the Division was stationed in the foothills of the Carpathian Mountains, becoming part of a Soviet Group formed for the invasion of Bessarabia. On 24 April 1941 it was converted into the 72nd Mountain Rifle Division.

Active Dates for the Great Patriotic War

None

Division Commanders

8.8.1940 - 24.4.1941 General-Major Pavel Ivlianovich ABRAMIDZE

Honors and Awards

None

Division Honorific Title

72nd Rifle Division

Divisional Units

214th Rifle Regiment
215th Rifle Regiment
216th Rifle Regiment
72nd Artillery Regiment

Assignments during the Great Patriotic War

None

72nd Rifle Division (II)

2nd Formation

The Division was formed on 15 December 1941 from cadre of the 7th Naval Infantry Brigade in 55th Army in Leningrad Front. The Division spent all of 1942 and 1943 defending along the Neva River with 55th, 2nd Shock and 42nd Armies. In January 1944 it participated in the Leningrad-Novgorod Offensive driving the Germans from the Leningrad area and winning its Honorific title and the Order of the Red Banner. The Division was then sent north and took part in the June Vyborg-Petrozavodsk Offensive knocking Finland out of the war. In July it was transferred south and participated in the Baltic Offensive with 8th Army in September/October 1944, clearing Estonia and the Baltic Islands. In October the Division was sent into STAVKA Reserves to rest and refit and was sent back to the front in December with 21st Army in 1st Ukrainian Front. In January the Division took part in the Vistula-Odor Offensive and in February/March the Lower and Upper Silesian Offensives. Finally, in May it participated in the Prague Operation ending the war as part of the Central Group of Forces in Czechoslovakia. The Division was ordered to disband in June 1945 and probably did sometime in July 1945. The number was not used again for a Rifle Division.

Active Dates for the Great Patriotic War

15 December 1941 – 4 October 1944
7 November 1944 – 30 November 1944
11 December 1944 – 11 May 1945

Division Commanders

15.12.1941 – 6.5.1942	General-Major Terentii Mikhailovich PARAFILLO
7.5.1942 – 11.5.1945	Colonel Il'ya Ivanovich YASTREBOV (promoted to General-Major on 26.9.1943)

Honors and Awards

22.1.1944	Awarded the Honorific designation "Pavlovskaia
26.2.1944	Awarded the Order of the Red Banner
22.6.1944	Awarded the Order of Suvorov II Class

Division Honorific Title

72nd Pavlovskaia Red Banner Order of Suvorov Rifle Division

Divisional Units

14th Rifle Regiment
133rd Rifle Regiment
187th Rifle Regiment
9th Artillery Regiment
119th Separate Antitank Artillery Battalion (formally 72nd Sep. Antitank Artillery battalion)
383rd Mortar Battalion (from 17.1.1942 to 15.10.1942)
40th Reconnaissance Company
3rd Sapper Battalion
5th Separate Signals Battalion (formally 480th Sep. Signals Company)
51st Medical Battalion
117th Separate Chemical Defense Company
120th Auto-Transport Company
347th Field Bakery
192nd Veterinary Field Hospital
1111th Field Postal Station
1133rd Field Cash Office of the State Bank

Operations

Sinyavino Army Group Offensive Operation	19.8.1942 - 10.10.1942
Mga Army Group Offensive Operation	15.9.1943 - 18.9.1944
Leningrad-Novgorod Strategic Offensive Operation	
Krasnoye Selo-Ropsha Army Group Offensive Operation	14.1.1944 - 30.1.1944
Kingisepp-Gdov Army Group Offensive Operation	1.2.1944 - 1.3.1944
Vyborg-Petrozavodsk Strategic Offensive Operation	
Vyborg Army Group Offensive Operation	10.6.1944 - 20.6.1944
Baltic Strategic Offensive Operation	
Tallin Army Group Offensive Operation	17.9.1944 - 26.9.1944
Moonzund Army Group Offensive Operation	5.10.1944 - 22.10.1944
Vistula-Odor Strategic Offensive Operation	
Sandomierz-Silesian Army Group Offensive Operation	12.1.1945 - 3.2.1945
Lower Silesian Army Group Offensive Operation	8.2.1945 - 24.2.1945
Upper Silesian Army Group Offensive Operation	15.3.1945 - 31.3.1945
Prague Strategic Offensive Operation	
Sudeten Army Group Offensive Operation	6.5.1945 - 11.5.1945

Assignments during the Great Patriotic War

Date	Front	Army	Corps
1 January 1942	Leningrad Front	55th Army	-
1 February 1942	Leningrad Front	55th Army	-
1 March 1942	Leningrad Front	55th Army	-

Date	Front	Army	Corps
1 April 1942	Leningrad Front	55th Army	-
1 May 1942	Leningrad Front	55th Army	-
1 June 1942	Leningrad Front	55th Army	-
1 July 1942	Leningrad Front	42nd Army	-
1 August 1942	Leningrad Front	42nd Army	-
1 September 1942	Leningrad Front	42nd Army	-
1 October 1942	Leningrad Front	55th Army	-
1 November 1942	Leningrad Front	55th Army	-
1 December 1942	Leningrad Front	55th Army	-
1943			
1 January 1943	Leningrad Front	55th Army	-
1 February 1943	Leningrad Front	55th Army	-
1 March 1943	Leningrad Front	55th Army	-
1 April 1943	Leningrad Front	55th Army	-
1 May 1943	Leningrad Front	55th Army	-
1 June 1943	Leningrad Front	55th Army	-
1 July 1943	Leningrad Front	55th Army	-
1 August 1943	Leningrad Front	55th Army	-
1 September 1943	Leningrad Front	2nd Shock Army	-
1 October 1943	Leningrad Front	2nd Shock Army	-
1 November 1943	Leningrad Front	42nd Army	-
1 December 1943	Leningrad Front	42nd Army	109th Rifle Corps
1944			
1 January 1944	Leningrad Front	42nd Army	109th Rifle Corps
1 February 1944	Leningrad Front	67th Army	110th Rifle Corps
1 March 1944	Leningrad Front	8th Army	115th Rifle Corps
1 April 1944	Leningrad Front	2nd Shock Army	109th Rifle Corps
1 May 1944	Leningrad Front	23rd Army	-
1 June 1944	Leningrad Front	21st Army	109th Rifle Corps
1 July 1944	Leningrad Front	21st Army	109th Rifle Corps
1 August 1944	Leningrad Front	2nd Shock Army	109th Rifle Corps
1 September 1944	Leningrad Front	8th Army	109th Rifle Corps
1 October 1944	Leningrad Front	8th Army	109th Rifle Corps
1 November 1944	STAVKA Reserves	21st Army	117th Rifle Corps
1 December 1944	STAVKA Reserves	21st Army	117th Rifle Corps
1945			
1 January 1945	1st Ukrainian Front	21st Army	117th Rifle Corps
1 February 1945	1st Ukrainian Front	21st Army	117th Rifle Corps
1 March 1945	1st Ukrainian Front	21st Army	117th Rifle Corps
1 April 1945	1st Ukrainian Front	21st Army	117th Rifle Corps
1 May 1945	1st Ukrainian Front	21st Army	117th Rifle Corps

Date	Front	Army	Corps
1 June 1945	Central Group of Forces	21st Army	117th Rifle Corps – ordered to disband

73rd Rifle Division (I)

1st Formation

The Division was formed in 1930 in Omsk in the Siberian Military District. It remained there throughout the 1930s. In August/September of 1939, as part of the partial mobilization conducted by the USSR, it was ordered to form two new Divisions, the 166th and 178th Rifle Divisions, based around two of the Divisions Rifle Regiments. What remained formed a new 73rd Rifle Division.

Active Dates for the Great Patriotic War

None

Division Commanders

Unknown

Honors and Awards

None

Division Honorific Title:

73rd Rifle Division

Divisional Units

217th Rifle Regiment
218th Rifle Regiment
219th Rifle Regiment
73rd Artillery Regiment

Assignments during the Great Patriotic War

None

73rd Rifle Division (II)

2nd Formation

The Division was formed in September 1939 from what remained of the original 73rd Rifle Division probably based around the 217th Rifle Regiment. The Division was disbanded in October 1939, although for what reason still remains unclear.

Active Dates for the Great Patriotic War

None

Division Commanders

Unknown

Honors and Awards

None

Division Honorific Title

73rd Rifle Division

Divisional Units

Unknown

Assignments during the Great Patriotic War

None

73rd Rifle Division (III)

3rd Formation

The Division was formed in July 1940 in Kalinin in the Moscow Military District. On 22 June 1941 the Division was in 20th Army in STAVKA Reserves at the peacetime 6,000 man strength. The Army was sent to the Western Front to form a new defensive line along the main route to Moscow, between Vitebsk and Orsha. Caught up in the battles around Smolensk, the Division was decimated. In October, still with 20th Army, it was encircled near Vyaz'ma during Operation Typhoon and destroyed. It was not officially disbanded until 27 December 1941.

Active Dates for the Great Patriotic War

2 July 1941 - 27 December 1941

Division Commanders

16.7.1940 - 27.12.1941	Colonel Aleksandr Ivanovich AKIMOV

Honors and Awards

None

Division Honorific Title

73rd Rifle Division

Divisional Units

392nd Rifle Regiment (I)
413th Rifle Regiment (I)
471st Rifle Regiment (I)
11th Artillery Regiment
148th Separate Antitank Artillery Battalion
469th Separate Antiaircraft Artillery Battalion
51st Reconnaissance Battalion
25th Sapper Battalion
78th Separate Signals Battalion
68th Medical Battalion
186th Auto-Transport Battalion

522nd Field Postal Station
440th Field Cash Office of the State Bank

Operations

The Battle of Smolensk
Smolensk Army Group Defensive Operation 10.7.1941 – 10.8.1941
Dukhovshchina Army Group Offensive Operation 17.8.1941 – 8.9.1941
Moscow Strategic Defensive Operation
Vyaz'ma army Group Defensive Operation 2.10.1941 – 13.10.1941

Assignments during the Great Patriotic War

Date	Front	Army	Corps
22 June 1941	STAVKA Reserves	20th Army	69th Rifle Corps
1 July 1941	STAVKA Reserves	20th Army	69th Rifle Corps
10 July 1941	Western Front	20th Army	-
1 August 1941	Western Front	20th Army	69th Rifle Corps
1 September 1941	Western Front	20th Army	-
1 October 1941	Western Front	20th Army	-

73rd Rifle Division (IV)

4th Formation

The Division was formed on 3 January 1942 in the North Caucasian Military District by renaming the 470th Rifle Division. In late May 1942, the Division was sent to the Southern Front to shore up the front line after the massive losses at Khar'kov. During the German drive on Stalingrad in the summer of 1942, the Division was forced to retreat and was destroyed by July. It was officially disbanded on 27 September 1942.

Active Dates for the Great Patriotic War

25 April 1942 – 27 September 1942

Division Commanders

3.1.1942 – 8.2.1942	Colonel Grigorii Matveevich KOCHENOV
9.2.1942 – 3.10.1942	Colonel Vasilii Vasil'evich GLAGOLEV

Honors and Awards

None

Division Honorific Title

73rd Rifle Division

Divisional Units

392nd Rifle Regiment (II)
413th Rifle Regiment (II)
471st Rifle Regiment (II)
11th Artillery Regiment
148th Separate Antitank Artillery Battalion
74th Separate Antiaircraft Artillery Battery
165th Mortar Battalion
51st Reconnaissance Company
25th Sapper Battalion
78th Separate Signals Battalion
68th Medical Battalion

457th Separate Chemical Defense Company
186th Auto-Transport Company
464th Field Bakery
929th Veterinary Field Hospital
1659th Field Postal Station
1106th Field Cash Office of the State Bank

Operations

Voronezh-Voroshilovgrad Strategic Defensive Operation
Voroshilovgrad-Shakhty Army Group Defensive Operation 7.7.1942 – 24.7.1942

Assignments during the Great Patriotic War

Date	Front	Army	Corps
1 January 1942	North Caucasian MD	-	-
1 February 1942	North Caucasian MD	-	-
1 March 1942	North Caucasian MD	-	-
1 April 1942	North Caucasian MD	-	-
1 May 1942	South Front	Front Reserves	-
1 June 1942	South Front	24th Army	-
1 July 1942	South Front	24th Army	-

73rd Rifle Division (V)

5th Formation

The Division was formed on 15 October 1942 in the 48th Army in Bryansk Front, from the cadre of the 122nd Separate Rifle Brigade and remained with 48th Army for the rest of the war. In March 1943, it was transferred to the Central Front. The Division was defending just north of the Kursk salient during the Battle of Kursk. In July, the Division participated in the Orel Offensive. In October 1943, it participated in the Byelorussian Strategic Offensive Operation, pushing the Germans back to the Dnepr in the area just south of Gomel. By this time (20.10.43) the Central Front had been renamed the Byelorussian Front. The Division also won its honorific during this action. In January 1944, it participated in the Kalinkovichi-Mozyr Army Group Operation, establishing a bridgehead over the Dnepr for future offensives. In June 1944, the Division participated in the Byelorussian Strategic Offensive Operation and the Lublin-Brest Offensive, advancing to the outskirts of Warsaw, and was awarded the Order of the Red Banner and the Order of Suvorov II class for its actions during these battles. In September of 1944, the 48th Army was transferred to 2nd Byelorussian Front. On 14 January 1945, the Division participated in the East Prussian Offensive which was its last offensive of the war. For its actions during this offensive the Division won the Order of Lenin. Although it was not designated to participate in the occupation of Poland as part of the Northern Group of Forces, it remained in Poland. And by November 1945, the Division had been returned to the USSR and was now located in the Don (later North Caucasus) Military District and assigned to the 29th Rifle Corps. It was reorganized in 1957 to the 73rd Mountain Rifle Division.

Active Dates for the Great Patriotic War

15 October 1942 – 9 May 1945

Division Commanders

15.10.1942 – 5.12.1943	Colonel Dmitrii Ivanovich SMIRNOV (promoted to General-Major on 18.5.1943)
6.12.1943 – 20.7.1944	Colonel Stepan Fedorovich PETROVSKII
21.7.1944 – 2.11.1944	Colonel Vasilii Ivanovich MATRONIN
3.11.1944 – 9.5.1945	Colonel Il'ya Mikhailovich PASHKOV (promoted to General-Major 5.5.1945)

Honors and Awards

2.10.1943	Awarded the Honorific designation "Novozybkovskaia"
2.7.1944	Awarded the Order of the Red Banner
25.7.1944	Awarded the Order of Suvorov II class
5.4.1945	Awarded the Order of Lenin

Division Honorific Title

73rd Novozybkovskaia Red Banner Order of Suvorov and Lenin Rifle Division

Divisional Units

392nd Rifle Regiment (III)
413th Rifle Regiment (III)
471st Rifle Regiment (III)
11th Artillery Regiment
148th Separate Antitank Artillery Battalion
51st Reconnaissance Company (formally 154th Reconnaissance Company)
25th Sapper Battalion (formally 196th Sapper Battalion)
358th Separate Signals Battalion (formally 625th and 613th Sep. Signals Companies)
68th Medical Battalion
54th Separate Chemical Defense Company (formally 15th Sep. Chemical Defense Company)
186th Auto-Transport Company (formally 185th Auto-Transport Battalion)
464th Field Bakery
929th Veterinary Field Hospital
1767th Field Postal Station
1724th Field Cash Office of the State Bank

Operations

Orel Strategic Offensive Operation	
Kromyv-Orel Army Group Offensive Operation	15.7.1943 - 18.8.1943
Chernigov-Poltava Strategic Offensive Operation	
Chernigov-Pripyet Army Group Offensive Operation	26.8.1943 - 30.9.1943
Byelorussian Strategic Offensive Operation	
Gomel'sko-Rechitskaia Army Group Offensive Operation	30.9.1943 - 30.10.1943
Gomel'sko-Rechitskaia Army Group Offensive Operation	10.11.1943 - 30.11.1943
Kalinkovichi Army Group Offensive Operation	8.12.1943 - 11.12.1943
Kalinkovichi Army Group Offensive Operation	20.12.1943 - 27.12.1943
Kalinkovichi-Mozyr Army Group Offensive Operation	8.1.1944 - 30.1.1944
Byelorussian Strategic Offensive Operation	
Bobruisk Army Group Offensive Operation	23.6.1944- 29.6.1944
Lublin-Brest Army Group Offensive Operation	18.7.1944 - 2.8.1944
East Prussian Strategic Offensive Operation	
Mlawo-Elbing Army Group Offensive Operation	14.1.1945 - 26.1.1945

Assignments during the Great Patriotic War

Date	Front	Army	Corps
1 November 1942	Bryansk Front	48th Army	-
1 December 1942	Bryansk Front	48th Army	-
1943			
1 January 1943	Bryansk Front	48th Army	-
1 February 1943	Bryansk Front	48th Army	-
1 March 1943	Bryansk Front	48th Army	-
1 April 1943	Central Front	48th Army	-
1 May 1943	Central Front	48th Army	-
1 June 1943	Central Front	48th Army	-
1 July 1943	Central Front	48th Army	-
1 August 1943	Central Front	48th Army	-
1 September 1943	Central Front	48th Army	-
1 October 1943	Central Front	48th Army	42nd Rifle Corps
1 November 1943	Byelorussian Front	48th Army	42nd Rifle Corps
1 December 1943	Byelorussian Front	48th Army	29th Rifle Corps
1944			
1 January 1944	Byelorussian Front	48th Army	-
1 February 1944	Byelorussian Front	48th Army	29th Rifle Corps
1 March 1944	Byelorussian Front	48th Army	29th Rifle Corps
1 April 1944	1st Byelorussian Front	48th Army	29th Rifle Corps
1 May 1944	1st Byelorussian Front	48th Army	29th Rifle Corps
1 June 1944	1st Byelorussian Front	48th Army	29th Rifle Corps
1 July 1944	1st Byelorussian Front	48th Army	53rd Rifle Corps
1 August 1944	1st Byelorussian Front	48th Army	29th Rifle Corps
1 September 1944	1st Byelorussian Front	48th Army	29th Rifle Corps
1 October 1944	2nd Byelorussian Front	48th Army	29th Rifle Corps
1 November 1944	2nd Byelorussian Front	48th Army	29th Rifle Corps
1 December 1944	2nd Byelorussian Front	48th Army	29th Rifle Corps
1945			
1 January 1945	2nd Byelorussian Front	48th Army	29th Rifle Corps
1 February 1945	2nd Byelorussian Front	48th Army	29th Rifle Corps
1 March 1945	3rd Byelorussian Front	48th Army	29th Rifle Corps
1 April 1945	3rd Byelorussian Front	48th Army	29th Rifle Corps
1 May 1945	3rd Byelorussian Front	48th Army	29th Rifle Corps

74th Rifle Division (I)

1st Formation

The Division was formed in 1924 based on cadre from the 22nd Rifle Division in the North Caucasus Military District. It remained there throughout the rest of the 1920s and the 1930s. In August/September of 1939, as part of the partial mobilization conducted by the USSR, it was ordered to form a new Division, the 157th Rifle Division, based around one of the Divisions Rifle Regiments. What remained formed a new 74th Rifle Division.

Active Dates for the Great Patriotic War

None

Division Commanders

28.2.1939 - ??.8.1939	Colonel Fedor Yefimovich SHEVERDIN

Honors and Awards

14.12.1926	Awarded the Honorific designation "Tamanskaia"

Division Honorific Title

74th Tamanskaia Rifle Division

Divisional Units

220th Rifle Regiment
221st Rifle Regiment
222nd Rifle Regiment
74th Artillery Regiment

Assignments during the Great Patriotic War

None

74th Rifle Division (II)

2nd Formation

The Division was formed in September 1939 in the North Caucasus Military District from what remained of the original 74th Rifle Division, probably based around the 220th Rifle Regiment. In the late fall of 1939, it was transferred north to the Leningrad Military District to take part in the war with Finland. It was probably one of the last Divisions designated to transfer home because in June 1940, it was transferred to the Odessa Military District to take part in the invasion of Bessarabia, Rumania.

On 22 June 1941 it was assigned to the 9th Separate Army defending along the border of Rumania. The Division retreated all the way back to the Don River bend by November 1941. After being transferred to 12th Army, it participated in the Rostov Offensive that pushed the Germans out of the city and stabilized the front line at the Mius River. In June 1942, as part of 12th Army, the Division was forced to retreat in the face of the German Offensive drive to Stalingrad and the Caucasus region. By August 1942, now in the 37th Army, the Division had lost so much personnel that the remaining men were transferred to other divisions within the Army. It was officially disbanded on 27 September 1942.

Active Dates for the Great Patriotic War

22 June 1941 - 27 September 1942

Division Commanders

??.8.1939 - 19.5.1942	Colonel Fedor Yefimovich SHEVERDIN (promoted to General-Major on 27.12.1941)
20.5.1942 - 26.5.1942	Unknown
27.5.1942 - 27.9.1942	Lieutenant-Colonel Ivan Mikhailovich BALENKO

Honors and Awards

Division carried all awards from the previous 74th Rifle Division

Division Honorific Title

74th Tamanskaia Rifle Division

Divisional Units

78th Rifle Regiment (I)
109th Rifle Regiment (I)
360th Rifle Regiment (I)
6th Artillery Regiment (until 14.7.1942)
81st Howitzer Artillery Regiment (until 15.11.1941)
142nd Separate Antitank Artillery Battalion
274th Separate Antiaircraft Artillery Battalion
111th Reconnaissance Battalion
110th Sapper Battalion
113th Separate Signals Battalion
19th Medical Battalion
111th Chemical Defense Company
16th Auto-Transport Battalion
11th Mobile Field Bakery
197th Field Postal Station
209th Field Cash Office of the State Bank

Operations

Moldavian Army Group Defensive Operation	1.7.1941 - 26.7.1941
Kiev Strategic Defensive Operation	
Tiraspol'-Melitopol Army Group Defensive Operation	27.7.1941 - 28.9.1941
Donbass-Rostov Strategic Defensive Operation	
Donbass Army Group Defensive Operation	29.9.1941 - 4.11.1941
Rostov Strategic Offensive Operation	
Bol'shekrepinsk Army Group Offensive Operation	17.11.1941 - 27.11.1941
Voronezh-Voroshilovgrad Strategic Defensive Operation	
Voroshilovgrad-Shakhty Army Group Offensive Operation	7.7.1942 - 24.7.1942
North Caucasian Strategic Defensive Operation	
Tikhoretsk-Stavropol' Army Group Defensive Operation	25.7.1941 - 5.8.1942
Armavire-Maikop Army Group Defensive Operation	6.8.1942 - 17.8.1942

Assignments during the Great Patriotic War

Date	Front	Army	Corps
22 June 1941	Separate Army	9th Army	48th Rifle Corps
1 July 1941	Southern Front	9th Army	48th Rifle Corps
10 July 1941	Southern Front	9th Army	48th Rifle Corps
1 August 1941	Southern Front	9th Army	48th Rifle Corps
1 September 1941	Southern Front	9th Army	-
1 October 1941	Southern Front	12th Army	-
1 November 1941	Southern Front	12th Army	-

Date	Front	Army	Corps
1 December 1941	Southern Front	12th Army	-
1942			
1 January 1942	Southern Front	12th Army	-
1 February 1942	Southern Front	12th Army	-
1 March 1942	Southern Front	12th Army	-
1 April 1942	Southern Front	12th Army	-
1 May 1942	Southern Front	12th Army	-
1 June 1942	Southern Front	12th Army	-
1 July 1942	Southern Front	12th Army	-
1 August 1942	North Caucasian Front	37th Army	-

74th Rifle Division (III)

3rd Formation

The Division was formed on 14 October 1942 in the 13th Army in Bryansk Front from cadre of the 134th Separate Rifle Brigade. It participated in the Soviet offensive that liberated Kursk and formed the famous salient. In March 1943, the 13th Army was transferred to Central Front and started preparing defensive positions north of Kursk. It took the brunt of the German 9th Army assault toward Ponyri. After halting the German offensive, the Soviets went over to the attack to liberate Orel. In late August to October 1943, the Division pushed the Germans back to the Dnepr River near Chernobyl'. Then in late October, the Division was transferred to the new 1st Ukrainian Front (formerly the Voronezh Front), and participated in the liberation of Kiev, winning its honorific title. In December 1943, it participated in the Zhitomir Offensive and the in the Korsun Offensive. Then in March 1944, it participated in the Uman-Botosani Offensive that push the Germans back to the Rumanian border. Next the Division took part in the Iasi-Kishinev Offensive that knocked Rumania out of the war, and then pushed into Bulgaria and captured Belgrade. The Division was transferred to 3rd Ukrainian Front in September 1944. In March 1945, it participated in the defensive near Lake Balaton and then took part in the advance to Vienna. After the war it remained part of the 26th Army of the Southern Group of Forces. When the 26th Army was withdrawn in 1946, the Division was disbanded.

Active Dates for the Great Patriotic War

14 October 1942 – 9 May 1945

Division Commanders

14.10.1942 - 7.10.1943	Colonel Andranik Abramovich KAZARYAN (promoted to General-Major on 22.2.1943)
8.10.1943 - 15.1.1944	Colonel Mikhail Dmitrievich KUZNETSOV
16.1.1944 - 5.10.1944	Lieutenant-Colonel Kutub Gainutdinovich GIZATULLIN (promoted to Colonel on 22.2.1944)
6.10.1944 - 17.11.1944	Colonel Konstantin Alekseevich SYCHEV
18.11.1944 - 9.5.1945	Colonel Fedor Ivanovich ZINOV'EV (promoted to General-Major 19.4.1945)

Honors and Awards

6.11.1943	Awarded the Honorific designation "Kiev"
4.1.1944	Awarded the Order of the Red Banner
24.4.1944	Awarded the Order of Bogdan Khmel'nitskiy II Class

Division Honorific Title

74th Kiev Red Banner Order of Bogdan Khmel'nitskiy Rifle Division

Divisional Units

78th Rifle Regiment (II)
109th Rifle Regiment (II)
360th Rifle Regiment (II)
6th Artillery Regiment
142nd Separate Antitank Artillery Battalion
111th Reconnaissance Company
110th Sapper Battalion
700th Separate Signals Battalion (formally 113th and 622nd Sep. Signals Companies)
19th Medical Battalion
111th Separate Chemical Defense Company
101st Auto-Transport Company
167th Field Bakery
67th Veterinary Field Hospital
1779th Field Postal Station
1736th Field Cash Office of the State Bank

Operations

Voronezh-Khar'kov Strategic Offensive Operation	
Voronezh-Kastornoye Army Group Offensive Operation	13.1.1943 – 2.2.1943
Orel (Maloarkhangl'sk Army Group Offensive Operation	5.2.1943 – 28.2.1943
Khar'kov Army Group Defensive Operation	4.3.1943 – 25.3.1943
Kursk Strategic Defensive Operation	
Orel-Kursk Army Group Defensive Operation	5.7.1943 – 11.7.1943
Orel Strategic Offensive Operation	
Kromyv-Orel Army Group Offensive Operation	15.7.1943 – 18.8.1943
Chernigov-Poltava Strategic Offensive Operation	
Chernigov-Pripyet Army Group Offensive Operation	26.8.1943 – 30.9.1943
Kiev Strategic Offensive Operation	
Chernobyl'-Radomysl' Army Group Offensive Operation	1.10.1943 – 4.10.1943
Chernobyl'-Gornostaipol Army Group Offensive Operation	3.10.1943 – 8.10.1943
Kiev Strategic Offensive Operation	3.11.1943 – 13.11.1943

Kiev Strategic Defensive Operation	13.11.1943 - 22.11.1943
Dnepr-Carpathian Strategic Offensive Operation	
Zhitomir-Berdichev Army Group Offensive Operation	24.12.1944 - 14.1.1944
Korsun-Shevchenkovsky Army Group Offensive Operation	24.1.1944 - 17.2.1944
Uman-Botosani Army Group Offensive Operation	5.3.1944 - 17.4.1944
Iasi-Kishinev Strategic Offensive Operation	
Iasi-Focsani Army Group Offensive Operation	20.8.1944 - 29.8.1944
Belgrade Strategic Offensive Operation	14.9.1944 - 24.11.1944
Budapest Strategic Offensive Operation	
Szekesfehervar-Esztergom Army Group Offensive Operation	20.12.1944 - 13.2.1945
Balaton Army Group Defensive Operation	6.3.1945 - 15.3.1945
Vienna Strategic Offensive Operation	
Veszprem Army Group Offensive Operation	16.3.1945 - 25.3.1945
Nagykanizsa-Kermand Army Group Offensive Operation	26.3.1945 - 15.4.1945
Assault on Vienna	4.4.1945 - 13.4.1945

Assignments during the Great Patriotic War

Date	Front	Army	Corps
1 November 1942	Bryansk Front	13th Army	-
1 December 1942	Bryansk Front	13th Army	-
1943			
1 January 1943	Bryansk Front	13th Army	-
1 February 1943	Bryansk Front	13th Army	-
1 March 1943	Bryansk Front	13th Army	-
1 April 1943	Central Front	13th Army	-
1 May 1943	Central Front	13th Army	-
1 June 1943	Central Front	13th Army	-
1 July 1943	Central Front	13th Army	15th Rifle Corps
1 August 1943	Central Front	13th Army	15th Rifle Corps
1 September 1943	Central Front	13th Army	15th Rifle Corps
1 October 1943	Central Front	13th Army	15th Rifle Corps
1 November 1943	1st Ukrainian Front	38th Army	21st Rifle Corps
1 December 1943	1st Ukrainian Front	40th Army	50th Rifle Corps
1944			
1 January 1944	1st Ukrainian Front	40th Army	50th Rifle Corps
1 February 1944	1st Ukrainian Front	40th Army	104th Rifle Corps
1 March 1944	2nd Ukrainian Front	40th Army	104th Rifle Corps
1 April 1944	2nd Ukrainian Front	40th Army	51st Rifle Corps

Date	Front	Army	Corps
1 May 1944	2nd Ukrainian Front	40th Army	50th Rifle Corps
1 June 1944	2nd Ukrainian Front	40th Army	50th Rifle Corps
1 July 1944	2nd Ukrainian Front	40th Army	50th Rifle Corps
1 August 1944	2nd Ukrainian Front	40th Army	50th Rifle Corps
1 September 1944	2nd Ukrainian Front	53rd Army	75th Rifle Corps
1 October 1944	3rd Ukrainian Front	57th Army	75th Rifle Corps
1 November 1944	3rd Ukrainian Front	57th Army	75th Rifle Corps
1 December 1944	3rd Ukrainian Front	57th Army	75th Rifle Corps
1945			
1 January 1945	3rd Ukrainian Front	57th Army	75th Rifle Corps
1 February 1945	3rd Ukrainian Front	26th Army	30th Rifle Corps
1 March 1945	3rd Ukrainian Front	26th Army	135th Rifle Corps
1 April 1945	3rd Ukrainian Front	26th Army	135th Rifle Corps
1 May 1945	3rd Ukrainian Front	26th Army	104th Rifle Corps
1 June 1945	Southern Group of Forces	26th Army	104th Rifle Corps

74th Rifle Division (IV)

4th Formation

The Division was formed 1956 in the Trans-Caucasus Military District when the 392nd Rifle Division was renumbered to the 74th Rifle Division. Shortly thereafter, it was transferred to the Siberian Military District where in 1957 it was reorganized to the 74th Motorized Rifle Division.

Division Commanders

Unknown

Honors and Awards

Division carried over awards from the 392nd Rifle Division
None awarded during 1955-1957

Division Honorific Title

74th Rifle Division

Divisional Units

Currently unknown, but probably same numbered Regiments as previous Division.

75th Rifle Division (I)

1st Formation

The Division was formed in 1927 in the Ukrainian Military District from cadre of the 25th Rifle Division. By 1939, it had been transferred north to the Leningrad Military District in Ostrov. It took part from the start in the war with Finland. After the war ended, the Division was transferred south to Mozyr' in the Western Special Military District. On 22 June 1941, the Division was in Western Front stationed along the Bug River near Brest. It retreated along the northern edge of the Pripyet Marshes and was transferred to 21st Army defending along the Dnepr River near Gomel. When 2nd Panzer Group turned south toward Kiev, the Division was forced to retreat and was caught in the encirclement near Kiev and destroyed in September. It was officially disbanded on 27 December 1941.

Active Dates for the Great Patriotic War

22 June 1941 - 27 December 1941

Division Commanders

22.6.1941 - 30.7.1941	Unknown*
30.7.1941 - 30.8.1941	Colonel Sergei Filippovich PIVOVAROV
31.8.1941 - ??.9.1941	Unknown*

* The commanders still remain unknown, most likely for political reasons.

Honors and Awards

None

Division Honorific Title

75th Rifle Division

Divisional Units

28th Rifle Regiment (formally 223rd Rifle Regiment)
34th Rifle Regiment (formally 224th Rifle Regiment)
115th Rifle Regiment (formally 225th Rifle Regiment)
68th Artillery Regiment (formally 75th Artillery Regiment)
235th Howitzer Artillery Regiment

82nd Separate Antitank Artillery Battalion
282nd Separate Antiaircraft Artillery Battalion
54th Reconnaissance Company
97th Sapper Battalion
75th Separate Signals Battalion
110th Medical Battalion
31st Separate Chemical Defense Company
69th Auto-Transport Battalion
49th Mobile Field Bakery
96th Divisional Artillery Workshop Battalion
300th Field Postal Station
106th Field Cash Office of the State Bank

Operations

Byelorussian Strategic Defensive Operation	
Border Defensive Battles	22.6.1941 - 25.6.1941
Battle of Smolensk	
Smolensk Army Group Defensive Operation	10.7.1941 - 10.8.1941
Gomel'-Trubchevsk Army Group Defensive Operation	24.7.1941 - 30.8.1941
Kiev Strategic Defensive Operation	
Kiev Priluki Army Group Defensive Operation	20.8.1941 - 26.9.1941

Assignments during the Great Patriotic War

Date	Front	Army	Corps
22 June 1941	Western Front	4th Army	28th Rifle Corps
1 July 1941	Western Front	4th Army	-
10 July 1941	Western Front	21st Army	-
1 August 1941	Central Front	3rd Army	66th Rifle Corps
1 September 1941	Bryansk Front	21st Army	66th Rifle Corps

75th Rifle Division (II)

2nd Formation

The Division was formed in on 8 January 1942 by renaming the 473rd Rifle Division in Baku, Trans-Caucasus Military District. The Division spent the entire war stationed in Iran as part of the inactive Army. When the Division withdrew from Iran in 1946, it remained assigned to the 4th Combined-Arms Army in the Bakin (later part of the Trans-Caucasus) Military District. It would remain there until 1957 when it was reorganized to the 75th Motorized Rifle Division, which would be disbanded late in 1957.

Active Dates for the Great Patriotic War

None

Division Commanders

8.1.1942 - 9.8.1942	Colonel Vasilii Leont'evich ABRAMOV
10.8.1942 - 18.5.1943	Colonel Timofei Ivanovich VOLKOVICH
19.5.1943 - 17.10.1943	Colonel Nikolai Denisovich RYZHOV
18.10.1943 - 1.11.1943	Colonel Semen Pavlovich STOROZHILOV
2.11.1943 - 9.5.1945	Colonel Nikolai Denisovich RYZHOV

Honors and Awards:

None

Division Honorific Title

75th Rifle Division

Divisional Units

34th Rifle Regiment
342nd Rifle Regiment
347th Rifle Regiment
124th Guards Artillery Regiment
1041st Separate Anti-Aircraft Artillery Battalion

Operations

None

Assignments during the Great Patriotic War:

Date	Front	Army	Corps
1 February 1942	Trans-Caucasian Military District	Armies in Iran	-
1 March 1942	Trans-Caucasian Military District	Armies in Iran	-
1 April 1942	Trans-Caucasian Military District	Armies in Iran	-
1 May 1942	Trans-Caucasian Military District	Armies in Iran	-
1 June 1942	Trans-Caucasian Front	Armies in Iran	-
1 July 1942	Trans-Caucasian Front	Armies in Iran	-
1 August 1942	Trans-Caucasian Front	Armies in Iran	-
1 September 1942	Trans-Caucasian Front	Armies in Iran	-
1 October 1942	Trans-Caucasian Front	Armies in Iran	-
1 November 1942	Trans-Caucasian Front	Armies in Iran	-
1 December 1942	Trans-Caucasian Front	Armies in Iran	-
1943			
1 January 1943	Trans-Caucasian Front	Armies in Iran	-
1 February 1943	Trans-Caucasian Front	Armies in Iran	-
1 March 1943	Trans-Caucasian Front	Armies in Iran	-
1 April 1943	Trans-Caucasian Front	Armies in Iran	-
1 May 1943	Trans-Caucasian Front	Armies in Iran	-
1 June 1943	Trans-Caucasian Front	Armies in Iran	-
1 July 1943	Trans-Caucasian Front	Armies in Iran	-
1 August 1943	Trans-Caucasian Front	Armies in Iran	-
1 September 1943	Trans-Caucasian Front	Armies in Iran	-
1 October 1943	Trans-Caucasian Front	Armies in Iran	-
1 November 1943	Trans-Caucasian Front	Armies in Iran	-
1 December 1943	Trans-Caucasian Front	Armies in Iran	-
1944			
1 January 1944	Trans-Caucasian Front	Armies in Iran	-
1 February 1944	Trans-Caucasian Front	4th Army	58th Rifle Corps
1 March 1944	Trans-Caucasian Front	4th Army	58th Rifle Corps
1 April 1944	Trans-Caucasian Front	4th Army	58th Rifle Corps
1 May 1944	Trans-Caucasian Front	4th Army	58th Rifle Corps
1 June 1944	Trans-Caucasian Front	4th Army	58th Rifle Corps
1 July 1944	Trans-Caucasian Front	4th Army	58th Rifle Corps

Date	Front	Army	Corps
1 August 1944	Trans-Caucasian Front	4th Army	58th Rifle Corps
1 September 1944	Trans-Caucasian Front	4th Army	58th Rifle Corps
1 October 1944	Trans-Caucasian Front	4th Army	58th Rifle Corps
1 November 1944	Trans-Caucasian Front	4th Army	58th Rifle Corps
1 December 1944	Trans-Caucasian Front	4th Army	58th Rifle Corps
1945			
1 January 1945	Trans-Caucasian Front	4th Army	58th Rifle Corps
1 February 1945	Trans-Caucasian Front	4th Army	58th Rifle Corps
1 March 1945	Trans-Caucasian Front	4th Army	58th Rifle Corps
1 April 1945	Trans-Caucasian Front	4th Army	58th Rifle Corps
1 May 1945	Trans-Caucasian Front	4th Army	58th Rifle Corps

Bibliography

Beloborodova, A. P. *et al,* **Voennie Kadre Sovetskogo Gosudarstva i Velikoi Otechestvennoi Voine 1941 – 1945 gg [Military Cadre of the Soviet State in the Great Patriotic War 1941 – 1945]**, Moscow, Boennoe Voennoe Izdatel'stvo Ministerstva Oboroni SSSR [Military Publishers of the Ministry of Defense of the USSR], 1963.

Glantz, David M., **Forgotten Battles of the German-Soviet War (1941-1945), Volumes III, IV, V,** Self Published, 1999, 2000

Gryler, A. N. *et al,* **Boevoi Sostav Sovetskii Armii, Chast I - V [Combat Composition of the Soviet Army, Volume I - V]**, Moscow, Voenno-Nauchnoe Upravlenie General'nogo Shtaba [Military History Directorate of the General Staff].

Kalashnikov, K. A. , *et al*, **Krasnaya Armiya v Iune 1941 goda [The Red Army in June 1941].** Tomsk, Tomsk State University Publishing House, 2001.

Lenskii, A. G., Tsybin, M. M.. **Pervaya sotnya: Strelkovye, Gornostrelkovye, Motostrelkovye, Motorizovannye Divizii RKKA Gruppy Nomerov 1-100 (1920-1945 gg.) Sprabochnik. [The First Hundred: Rifle, Mountain, Motorized Rifle, Motorized Divisions of the RKKA numbers group 1-100 (1920-1945) Handbook.]** Saint-Petersburg, 2003.

Markheva, V. I. Major *et al,* **Komandovanie Korpusnogo i Divizionnogo Zvena Sovetskikh Vooruzhennikh Sil Perioda Velikoi Otechestvennoi Voini 1941 – 1945 gg. [Commanders of the Corps and Divisional Units of the Soviet Armed Forces in the Period of the Great Patriotic War 1941 – 1945]**, Moscow, Military Academy in the name of M. V. Frunze, 1964.

Unknown Authors. **Perechen No. 5: Strelkovykh, Gornostrelkovykh, Motostrelkovykh I Motoizovannykh Divizii, Vkhodiviikh v Sostav Deistvuyuschei Armii v gody Velikoi Otechestvennoi Voiny 1941 – 1945 gody. [List No. 5: Rifle, Mountain Rifle, Motorized Rifle and Motorized Divisions, included in the Composition of the Active Army in the years of the Great Patriotic War 1941 – 1945.]** Moscow, 1956.

Fes'kov, V. I. Kalashnikov, K. A., Golikov, V. I.. **Sovetskaya Armiya v Gody "Kholodnoi Voiny" (1945 – 1991)[The Soviet Army in the Years of the "Cold War" (1945 – 1991)]**. Tomsk, Tomsk University Publishing, 2004.

Dimaggio, Adam. **Orders and Medals of the USSR**. http://www.acadiacom.net/adimag/index.html

Ivlev, Igor' I.. **Soldat [Soldiers]**. http://www.soldat.ru.

www.ingramcontent.com/pod-product-compliance
Ingram Content Group UK Ltd.
Pitfield, Milton Keynes, MK11 3LW, UK
UKHW051128260726
13967UKWH00010B/2920

9 780972 029605